Business and Fundamentals of Music Production

First Edition

Circa 1996 Los Angeles Larrabee Recording Studios – Heavy D and Tony Dofat producing the RIAA certified gold album "Waterbed Hev"

Illustration by: Timothy "TJ" Mahon

Business and Fundamentals of
Music Production

Tony M Dofat

TDC Group, Inc.
New York, NY
TDC
2016

First Printing: 2016

ISBN 978-0-578-17904-9

TDC Group, Inc.

www.thetdcgroupinc com

For special orders, please call (646) 402-5519

Contact: tony@thetdcgroupinc.com

Dedication

This book is dedicated to my good friend Dwight "Heavy-D" Myers. May you sleep in peace my friend and thank you for your inspiration and motivation to write this book. To my nephew Derek "Chan" Richardson, my family, and my 4 sons.

Contents

Acknowledgements

I'd like to thank a few professionals, Institutes, and Industry greats throughout my tenure in the recording arts Industry including;

Sean "Puffy" Combs, Harve Pierre, Bad Boy Worldwide, Heavy-D, Tony Maserati, Bob "Bassy" Brockmann, Prince Charles Alexander, Roey Shamir, Richard Keller, Francis Manzella, Chris Athens, Chris Gehringer, Gregory Trotman, Tony Drootin, Deborah Mannis-Gardner & DMG Clearances, Inc, Rob Chiarelli, Rich Travali, Rob Paustian, Kenyatta Beasley, Nikki Turner, SAE Institute, IAR Institute, Berklee College of Music, Long Island University, The TDC Group, Inc. roster and staff, Engine Room Audio, Sterling Sound Mastering, Area 51 Studios NYC, The Hit Factory and my nephew Timothy Mahon.

(This page was intentionally left blank)

Preface

This book contains everything you need to know about the business of music production from the creative aspect or publishing your own music to working with major record labels and creating your own boutique independent label. Music production is more than a hobby, this outlet has created a plethora of self-made Multi Millionaires and I have documented the manual to become the next Music Mogul. This textbook was written to dissect commercial record production and guide the next young and passionate musicians to the road of music success. My inspiration for writing this textbook developed during the midst of my mentoring and while allowing record label interns and assistants to shadow my work.

Introduction

Reminiscing back, 25 years ago when I was a newbie in the music industry, I often ask myself, "How did I become a music producer?" Prior to becoming a producer, I didn't know what a producer was and had no clue as to what were the duties of a music producer. It was my Passion! My passion for creating music and for making something from nothing. Music producers are mostly the brains behind a lot of these recording artists careers but was always overlooked, early on. As the times changed, so did the curiosity of the fans, questioning who produced this hit record and who produced that record. From the 80's, music producers slowly climbed into the forefront and were viewed as the man behind the man. This book will teach and guide you through your production path, from novice to the next hit maker. We will cover everything there is to know about becoming a music producer, legally, creatively, and being able to turn a hobby into a career.

(This page was intentionally left blank)

Chapter 1

What is a Music Producer

Overview

> * Defining a Music Producer
> * Job Description of a Producer
> * Responsibilities of a Producer
> * Producing a song from start to finish

There are well over 8,000 genres of music in the world today, some have a more broader appeal to a larger audience and more popular than others. The genres that are most common are considered mainstream or commercial music and are very profitable which helped contribute to this billion-dollar industry. These genres that can generate a reasonable amount of revenue are then recorded, manufactured, packaged, promoted, marketed, and then sold to the consumer. There are a few vehicles and necessary steps to transform musical ideas into tangible products. One of these main vehicles is known as a music producer. This chapter will explain in detail exactly what a music producer does and how powerful this person behind the scenes influence the world with the music we hear today, from radio, television, concerts and product branding.

The word, Producer, is commonly heard throughout the music industry but what exactly is a producer? When we are referring to music and making records, a producer is one who produces or creates music of course. I've watched this job title become more and more popular with time but very few actually knows the duties or job description of a music producer. Some people often mistake or confuse musicians, beat makers, programmers, or audio engineers with music producers, which at times you can be all but not necessarily always true. As a music producer, you are responsible for taking just an idea or song concept and delivering a finished product known as the Master Recording to the hiring company or client (the record label). Producers are Considered the directors of music, somewhat like directors in film and are creative and technical at the same time and are usually hired by the record company or recording artist and chosen due to their expertise and caliber of knowing how to make or [produce] commercially satisfactory music. In other situations, music producers will find undiscovered talent then develop them and present them to a record company with hopes of securing a recording contract for the artist. The record company will usually sign an artist being solicited by producers contingent upon the producer's track record and experience.

As a music producer, your main tools are your ears. You may not touch any buttons or faders but you may still have the capability to produce a #1 song. You are also the session leader and take full responsibility and control of everything from start to finish. You are usually the first person to walk in the studio and the last one to leave for each session. Producers must coordinate and designate studio sessions until the master track is delivered to the client or record company.

Some of the duties and tasks of a producer

- Creating and overseeing the budget
- Hiring songwriters
- Hiring composers
- Hiring arrangers
- Hiring background vocalists
- Hiring a vocal coach or vocal arranger
- Hiring musicians
- Hiring programmers
- Hiring recording engineers
- Hiring mixing engineers

Music producers will also hire any other necessary personnel that may be needed in order to complete the vision of the song. As mentioned earlier, most times in R&B and Hip-Hop, producers will Usually handle 2 or 3 of these duties but keep in mind; this may not always be the case.

While recording studio vocals, it is the producer's job to approve the vocals, consisting of a melody and lyrics. You will also approve the vocal performance of the recording artist. Music producers will also direct and coach the vocalist or artist while recording the vocals and determine if the artist needs to retake or re record some lines or phrases over. It's your job to Suggest harmony arrangements and whether or not to add background vocals to the song. On some occasions, the vocal directing sessions may not be the producer's strong points so professional vocal arrangers or vocal producers may be hired to complete this duty. You may not be as fluent with technical terms such as; vibrato, crescendo, flat or sharp but you'll know immediately if something doesn't sound correct. This will be enough to make your decision whether or not you'd like to re record that particular segment again.

During the recording or music tracking process of instruments and drums, the producer usually determines the patch or keyboard sound as well as the drum kit or drum sound and style to be recorded. In the final mixing stage, the producer will sit with the mix engineer and adjust frequencies of sounds and volumes of each individual track or instrument. It is also common for a producer to suggest adding effects or dynamics to vocal and instruments tracks making each track gel together as one complete song. At times, the producer may edit or rearrange the song while in it's final stage of production to improve the final vision.

As a producer, you will announce the start and stop of the recording for each segment or take and determine if it's good or acceptable. Directing the musicians is somewhat similar to directing vocals.

Making sure the Musicians play with the appropriate feel and vibe to fit the song is important. If your goal is to produce a slow, meaningful Love song, your musicians must be directed to play accordingly and it's the producer's job to set the mood and determine if their performance was acceptable.

Producer responsibilities

- Designate time and studio to record - This is usually handled by a production coordinator Within the production company or record label but is the producer's responsibility to choose the recording facility, time, and dates of the recording sessions.
- Budget forecast - The producer must forecast an exact dollar amount for the costs to record and deliver the master recording. The budget must be itemized and any expenses that may be incurred, including but not limited to studio time costs, equipment rental fees, ground transportation, lodging, flights, musician fees, background vocalist fees, supplies (disks, CD's, etc.), and any other necessities.
- Hire personnel - It is the producer's responsibility to find and hire the musicians, Songwriters, engineers, Mixers, composers, arrangers and any other necessary work for hire that may be needed to complete the master recording.
- Lyric sheet - Producer must deliver lyric sheets for the songs recorded.
- Sample sheet - Producer must supply information regarding any sample use if necessary. The information would be used for the label's licensing and clearing department.
- Master delivery - Producer must deliver completed, commercially satisfactory stereo masters and the label or executive producer of the project must approve them.
- Session logs - Producer must fill out session logs containing writers information, publishing information, background vocalists,

And any other parties that contributed to the masters. This purpose is to eliminate any third party claims and publishing disputes.

- Credits - Producer is responsible for deliver of full song credits, this will appear in the liner notes of CD's

Below is a flow chart explaining the steps in delivering a song, from inception to retail. All documents and fully mixed song shall be delivered during the "Label Approval" stage.

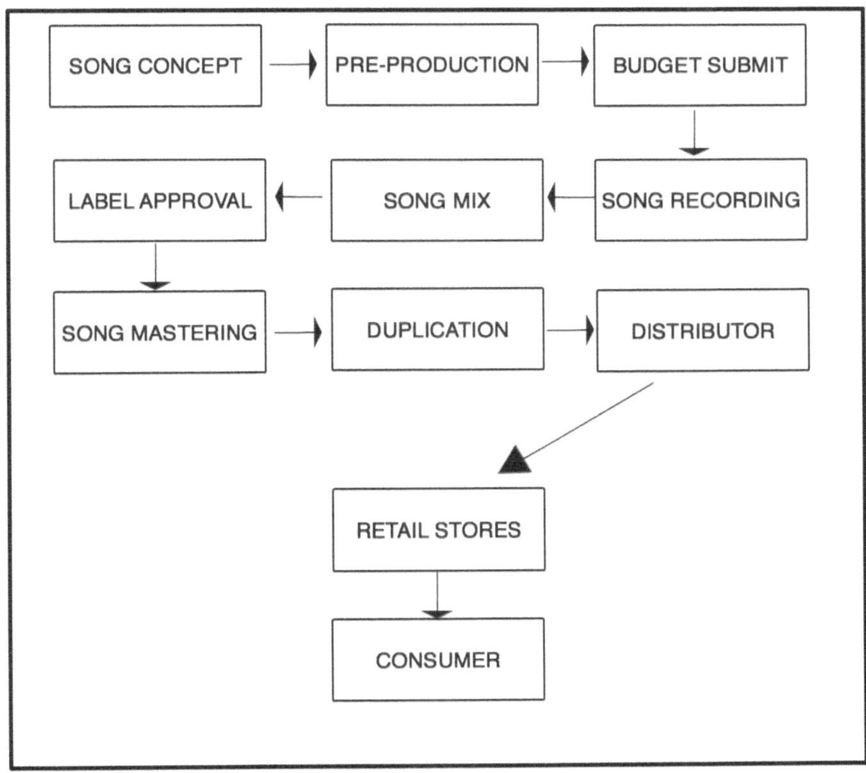

Chapter 2

Terms of Music Production

Advance – Money given to an artist or producer "up-front" and then later deducted or recouped from future sales of units.

AFM – American Federation of Musicians is a union for musicians. There is a local chapter for each state or region. The chapter for NY is Local 802.

AFTRA – American Federation of television and radio artists is a performers union for background vocalists.

Analog – Analog is the opposite of digital. Any technology, such as vinyl records or clocks with hands and faces, that doesn't break everything down into binary code to work.

Bit rate - The number of bits that pass a given point in a telecommunication network in a given amount of time, usually a second. Thus, a bit rate is usually measured in some multiple of bits per second - for example, kilobits, or thousands of bits per second (Kbps). A higher bit rate equals to a higher quality of audio or video.

Breach - an act of breaking or failing to observe a law, agreement, or code of conduct.

Cease and desist - known as "infringement letter" or "demand letter," is a document sent to an individual or business to halt purportedly unlawful activity ("cease") and not take it up Again later ("desist"). The letter may warn that if the recipient by deadlines set in the letter does not cease and desist specified conduct, or take certain actions, that party may be sued.

Copyright - the exclusive legal right, given to an originator or an assignee to print, publish, perform, film, or record literary, artistic, or musical material, and to authorize others to do the same.

DAW – Digital Audio Workshops used for the production of music, radio, television, podcasts, multimedia and nearly any other situation where complex recorded audio is needed, for example; Protools, Logic, Reason, Etc.

Deal Memorandum - Deal Memos are the term that producers use for employment contracts. Since the word "contract" implies something legally detailed and binding, the term "memo" is used to suggest an agreement somewhat less formal. Do not be mislead; a "Deal Memo" is a contract and is binding.

Digital – Sometimes referred to as digital audio is a method of representing sound as numerical values. This differs from analog media such as magnetic tapes or vinyl records for instance where the sound is stored in a physical form. In the case of cassette tapes, this information is stored magnetically.

Audio Engineer - An audio engineer works with the technical aspects of sound during the processes of recording, mixing, and re-production. Audio engineers often assist record producers and musicians to help give their work the sound they are hoping to achieve.

Interpolation - An interpolation is a replayed piece of a recording meant to sound exactly the same as the recording to avoid copyright clearances. It usually gives credit to the authors of the work but not to the performers of the original recording.

Master – A stereo 2 track of your final recording presented in a master format for duplication purposes in either an analog ½" tape or high quality digital format.

Mix Engineer - A mix engineer or mixing engineer is a person responsible for combining ("mixing") the different sonic elements of a piece of recorded music (vocals, instruments, effects etc.) into a final version of a song (also known as "final mix" or "mix down").

Monetize - To monetize is to convert an asset into or establish something as money or legal tender. The term monetize has different meanings depending on the context. It can refer to methods utilized to generate profit, while it also can literally mean the conversion of an asset into money.

Non-destructive Recording - Non-destructive recording is a method of recording where new takes or tracks are recorded while preserving the previously recorded tracks.

Non-linear Editing - Non-linear editing/recording typically refers to computer-based systems that allow any parts of the recording to be played back in any order with no gaps. Conventional tape is

Referred to as linear, because the material can only play back in the order in which it was recorded. Describes digital recording systems that allow any parts of the recording to be played back in any order with no gaps. Conventional tape is referred to as linear, because the material can only play back in the order in which it was recorded.

Overdubs - Record (additional sounds) on an existing recording.

Performance Rights Organizations - A performance rights organization (PRO), also known as a performing rights society, provides intermediary functions, particularly collection of royalties, between copyright holders and parties who wish to use copyrighted works publicly in locations such as shopping and dining venues. You may know these organizations as ASCAP, BMI, and SESAC.

Plug-in – Also known as an add-in, add-on, or extension is a software component that adds a specific feature to an existing computer program. When a program supports plug-ins, it enables customization which enhances your primary or another software.

Publishing - Music publishing can best be defined as the act of assigning particular legal rights, and a percentage of any income a song or musical composition might generate, to an individual or a company, for a specified period of time.

Quantization – The process of aligning a set of musical notes to a precise setting or tempo map. This results in notes being set on beats and on exact fractions of beats. The most frequent application of quantization in this context lies within MIDI application software or hardware.

Record Label - Record labels are companies that manufacture and distribute recorded music and promote that music.

Recoup - to get back money that you have spent or lost. Advances, production costs, marketing and promotions are some examples of recoupable expenses by a record label.

Royalty - A payment to an owner for the use of property, copyrighted works, franchises or natural resources. A royalty payment is Made to the legal owner of a property, patent, copyrighted work or franchise by those who wish to make use of it for the purposes of Generating revenue or other such desirable activities. In most cases, royalties are designed to compensate the owner for the asset's use.

Royalties pertaining to record sales are usually scaled as a "point" system.

Sample - In music, sampling is the act of taking a portion, or sample, of one sound recording and reusing it as an instrument or a sound recording in a different song or piece resulting into a new copyright.

Sample rate – A sample rate is the number of samples of a sound that are taken per second to represent the event digitally. The more samples taken per second, the more accurate the digital representation of the sound can be. For example, the current sample rate for CD-quality audio is 44,100 samples per second. This sample rate can accurately reproduce the audio frequencies up to 20,500 hertz, covering the full range of human hearing.

Song Bridge - The Bridge is often used to contrast with and prepare for the return of the verse and the chorus. "The b section of the popular song chorus is often called the bridge or release." For example, the B of AABA in thirty-two-bar form, with the verse surrounding the whole. The bridge is usually the climax of a song.

Song hook or chorus - The term "hook" likely goes back to the earliest days of songwriting because it refers to the part of the song intended to "hook" the listener: a catchy combination of melody, lyrics and rhythm that stays in the listener's head — something that songwriters from the dawn of time have wanted to achieve. The hook or chorus is the most familiar and most repetitious part of a song.

Song vamp – A vamp is the repeated use of a phrase through an entire song or the improvisation on top of a repeated phrase through a song.

Songwriter – A person who writes music, words, or music and words for a song.

Split sheet – A split sheet allows for all creative parts of a song to document their contribution and publishing share to avoid possible publishing and copyright disputes in the future.

Vocal Producer – Sometimes known as a vocal coach or the person in charge of directing the artist or studio vocalist while recording. The producer originally performed this duty until the late 90's.

VST – Known as Virtual Studio Technology (VST) is a software interface that integrates software audio synthesizer and effect plugins with audio editors and recording systems. VST and similar technologies use digital signal processing to simulate traditional recording studio hardware in software.

Chapter 3

Positions of Music Production

Assistant Engineer

Assistant engineer's main duties are to assist or help the engineer and are hired by the recording studio. Starting out as an intern and fresh out of college, an assistant engineer must earn his or her stripes to advance. You must know the analytics of the recording studio somewhat like the back of your hand and must be familiar with microphone setups for live drum kits and instruments, patch bay configuration, analog tape machines including analog outboard gear in addition to the most frequently used DAWs. Even after being promoted to an assistant engineer's position, occasionally you still may have to make a quick store run, order food, or brew the next pot of fresh coffee. In return, you will have the pleasure and advantage to learn and work under some of the best audio engineers and producers in the business. You will also receive liner note credit for the projects in which you work on as well as Grammy recognition and RIAA certified gold/platinum plaques if your projects are successful. You are paid an hourly wage by the recording studio and sometimes a bonus or perks from the client if you are exceptionally great and likeable.

Engineer

Taking on the role of an engineer, you are in charge of the audio quality among a list of other things and/or considered the link or liaison between the producer and the recording technology. It is your

Decision on the brand and model of microphone used for recording, as well as microphone pre amp, compressor, microphone chain, Monitors, bit-rate, sample rate, and anything dealing with the outcome of the song sonically. You are pretty much freelance at this stage of your Audio career and can earn anywhere between $25-$100 per hour, depending on your experience and track record. Most engineers build close relationships with their clients or recording artists and sometimes can even enter into exclusive "work for hire" contracts earning an easy six-figure salary as a staff or chief engineer.

Mix Engineer

This is the third stage of your audio career and you will more than likely engineer in conjunction with being a mix engineer. You are responsible for creating a final 2 track final mix down by blending each individual sound and track to make 1 stereo composite, which will eventually be sent to a mastering house and then the record label. You must be well experienced with analog outboard gear as well as plug-in usage, dynamics, reverbs, delays, and multi-effect processors. You will work very closely with the producer during the mix down stage and can make or break the song. Mixers are usually paid per day or per song, depending on your experience and demand. Sometimes, you may even qualify for a royalty if you are superb with numerous hits beneath your belt. You are considered a professional at this stage of your career.

Musicians

As a musician, you are hired by the producer and usually chosen by your level of expertise and your style of playing. You are more than likely a member of the musicians union (AFM) and paid according to your union scale. Union pay is determined by the song length, amount of tracks or overdubs, also the length of time you're at the studio. If you are a session leader you are also paid more. Most times,

Musicians have great relationships with the producers and only charge a flat fee at times.

Background vocalists

All background vocalists are hired by the producer and your job is based on your speed of performance, voice training, voice texture, and mostly by relationships or contacts. As a background vocalist, you are more than likely a member of AFTRA, which is similar to the musician's Union and is paid according to their policies and Scale. As with musicians, vocalists may have relationships with producers and only charge a flat fee as well.

Vocal producer

The vocal producer job was created around the late 90's and your sole purpose as a vocal producer is to record and direct the vocalists or artist to capture the best vocal take possible, which is satisfactory to the producer. In the earlier days, vocal producers were Named vocal coaches and most artists used them for note accuracy. Vocal producers are common in today's music production and their fees are usually a flat, 1 time fee per song.

Vocal Editor

A vocal editor was created in the mid 2000's with the boom of a program called Melodyne by the company Celemony. Melodyne is pitch correction and modification software similar to Antares Auto-tune. Melodyne is way more flexible and more natural sounding than Auto-tune but more difficult to use and very time consuming. Most times, producers will pass along the vocal tracks to a vocal editor that specializes in Melodyne to perfect all of the vocal tracks. The producer or engineer would then import the edited vocal tracks back into the master session for perfect pitched and flawless vocals.

Music Programmer

Many times, producers will call on programmers or sound designers to create that special patch or to sequence drum patterns. Most producers usually start their careers as programmers or beat makers

Until they're skilled enough to produce music on their own. Programmers will use their DAW of choice and will usually sit behind a studio desk with Headphones designing drum kits or drum patterns for the producer to review as an addition to their current project or perhaps future projects.

Interns

Most producers and recording studios hire interns, which mostly consist of students or graduates from a post secondary music institution. Interns would start out from the bottom as runners and gradually work their way up to a paid position. There will be a lot of coffee making and store running at the beginning of your internship.

Songwriter

Songwriters are the first to get hired by the producer and is usually brought in on a partnership basis where they would split the writer's share equally, 50% each. They are responsible for the words, melody, and also the reference vocal for the demo. Sometimes the writers may ask for an up-front fee for their time but depending upon your relationship, most will just collaborate for their publishing share.

Chapter 4

The Recording Budget

Overview

- What is a recording budget
- The purpose of a recording budget
- Reasonable costs associated with recording

Once a producer is hired by a label and prior to recording with the artist, the label or A&R Administration department usually requires a written budget, which needs approval before any money is spent. This budget is just a forecast or ballpark figure for the safety and concerns of the artist and accounting and recoupment. 100% of this budget will be recouped against the artist's royalties so it is thoroughly reviewed by the management team or artist's business manager. Below is an example of a budget for one song; it must contain any and all expected expense in detail. If the producer exceeds the budget, most times they are responsible to cover any overages.

Only associated costs pertaining to the production of the project are acceptable and if there are costs in which the Executive Producer deem unnecessary, your budget will get rejected. Travel, Ground transportation, supplies, per Diem, food, Etc. are all acceptable and reasonable. Clothes, sneakers, jewelry, personal items or household items are example of things, which aren't acceptable.

Let us take this following budget example and break it down. According to this detailed budget, it will cost the label $31,199 to produce one master. Labels stipulate within the artist's recording contract that they will only pay to record 10 masters, if you decide to record more than 10 masters then you, the artist must pay out of

Pocket for them. If you multiply this budget by 10 songs, the label will pay a minimum of $311,990 to complete the production of the Entire album project, pursuant to the contract. Every penny spent will be recouped against the artist's royalties so ultimately, the artist is Paying for their own album and the label is basically extending a loan with hopes to sell units.

There are times where you may have to submit several budgets because the label may not be willing to spend $311,990 for a new artist. Sometimes the producers may have to cut their fee or maybe use a less expensive recording facility. Many new artists have caps on their budgets at $25,000 maximum per song. The more popular selling artists sometimes will have a $50,000 cap or even more because it is more likely for the more popular artist to sell more units and in return the risk factor will be less. There are also times where the Executive Producer may want to change the direction of the project mid-way during the recording process, which means that some songs will more than likely get shelved indefinitely so they may request a reforecast of the budget to allocate more funds for the purpose of recording more material. This is another expense in which the artist will be responsible for and recouped from their sales.

In 2015, recording budgets for new artists have dramatically decreased due to the simplicity of the recording process and track making. Artists are now delivering finished products and the labels and distributors are simply buying the finished product, in return, the artists receives a small advance. Similar to any start-up or project, forecasting a budget is always the safest route and will never become a thing of the past. It is best to see what's expected to spend as opposed to completing only 75% of your project due to the unexpected depletion of your funds.

Below is an actual song budget, which was approved. Use this as a guide prior to starting your next project.

Recording Budget

Artist: Mary J Blige
Producer: Tony Dofat & Puffy
Song Title: TBA
Date: 3/14/96

PRE-PRODUCTION	>>>>>>>>>>>>		$0
PRODUCER ADVANCE	>>>>>>>>>>>>		$17,000.00
STUDIO			
Recording	30 hrs x $125 per	>>>>>>>>>	$3,750.00
Overdubs	12 hrs x $125 per	>>>>>>>>>	$1,500.00
Mixing	20 hrs x $125 per	>>>>>>>>>	$2,500.00
Total Studio		>>>>>>>>>	**$7,750.00**
ENGINEER			
Recording	30 hrs x $50 per	>>>>>>>>>	$1,500.00
Overdubs	12 hrs x $50 per	>>>>>>>>>	$600.00
Mixing	$1,500 FLAT FEE	>>>>>>>>>	$1,500.00
Total Engineer		>>>>>>>>>	**$3,600.00**
SUPPLIES			
Hard Drive	$249.00	>>>>>>>>>	$249.00
(12) CD's	10 x $5 per	>>>>>>>>>	$50.00
Total Supplies		>>>>>>>>>	**$299.00**
GROUND TRANSPORTATION			
3 round-trips for the artist	$100/ea	>>>>>>>>>	$300.00
5 round-trips for the producer	$100/ea	>>>>>>>>>	$500.00
Total Ground		>>>>>>>>>	**$800.00**
LODGING	>>>>>>>>>>>>>>>		$0
STUDIO RENTALS			
Misc	$750.00	>>>>>>>>>	$750.00
Total Rentals		>>>>>>>>>	**$750.00**
		GRAND TOTAL	**$30,199.00**

Chapter 5

Production Agreements

A major part in music production is the business or the agreement stages. This chapter will cover the legal paperwork regarding the production of a song. Contracts will outline everyone's obligations, compensation, and term or length. I will show you illustrations but let me explain first; A Deal memo or deal memorandum will be introduced first. The purpose of the deal memo is to have something legally binding where both parties agree upon key factors of the deal:

- **Term:** The length of your contract's initial (first) period
- **Obligation**: This will detail your commitment and will defer any payments owed to you if your services are not provided fully.
- **Compensation**: Your producer advance or fee in which you are entitled to for your services rendered.
- **Royalty:** Your percentage or equity in the project after the label has recouped. These figures are calculated by the point system.
- **Sample Usage**: This will determine who will be responsible for the sample(s) if any. Advance, Royalty, and licensing fee responsibility.

Once these key paragraphs are agreed upon, the next agreement, which will be presented to you by the label or hiring company is called a producer's declaration.

The producer Declaration is usually a one sheet memo and just states that you are the creator of the music and will take full responsibility of that particular song or songs keeping the label free of any third party claims or copyright infringement, and you are the sole owner of that song and also have full authority to record it for the "Artist" and grant usage to the "label". The declaration is straightforward with about 7-10 paragraphs and are rarely negotiated.

Once you sign your deal memo and producer declaration, you will have to fill out the proper tax forms prior to receiving your advance which we will discuss in the next chapter call "producer advance and royalties" I have learned this from decades of experience so I would suggest that you hire a lawyer to look over your deal memo and declaration, not to be alarmed but you should never sign anything without representation. This shouldn't cost much as most entertainment lawyers charge by the amount of work and hours are put into a specific contract and deal memos, short form agreements are usually just 1 to 5 pages long.

Choosing a great attorney should always come from a referral and most good attorneys are. Prior to attorneys committing to take you on as a client, they will have you sign a document called a retainer, which is simple and dry, cut. It outlines your attorney client privilege, their monthly fee, and their hourly fee. When an attorney is on retainer, all legal correspondence will go directly to them and they should alert you prior to working on anything on your behalf. Sometimes attorneys may charge a percentage if you are entering into larger deals such as, co-publishing, label deal, or a recording contract directly with a major label. Never hire an attorney from a television commercial and make sure they practice entertainment law, as you know that all laws are totally different.

After the attorney reviews your execution copies of your producers deal memo and Producer declaration, the label will then release your payment and will begin the project. During your creative stages or the song and while on the road to completion, the label's business affairs department is preparing the actual "long form" agreement (The official 30 page contract) between the producer and the label. Sometimes, these contacts cant take months to negotiate and I've watch some contacts fall apart because both sides are stubborn, thus the reason why you may not hear certain songs on commercial albums for retail but you will hear them on mixtapes, unreleased leaks or exclusives.

The following are some examples of actual deal memos or short form producer agreement, producer declarations, and Attorney's retainers. If you are unfamiliar with some of the legal terms and language, please refer to the "definitions" in chapter 2 or the glossary in the back of this book. It is ideal for a producer to understand these simple agreements to make sure your attorney or management is doing their job and also to understand certain clauses while your attorney is reviewing your contracts with you. If you don't understand something, make sure to stop and ask the attorney to further explain.

Tony M Dofat

PRODUCER DECLARATION

I hereby certify that I have produced or will have produced certain master recordings (individually and collectively, the "Master") embodying the performance of **XXXXXX** (hereinafter "Artist") pursuant to an agreement ("Producer Agreement") between **XXXXXXXX** ("Company") and I, which provides for valuable consideration to be paid to me. As part of my material obligations pursuant to the Producer Agreement and for the express and direct benefit of the Company and their licensees and assigns, I hereby:

1.   Grant to Company the perpetual right to use and publish and to permit others to use and publish my name, signatures, approved likeness, and approved biographical material concerning myself for advertising and trade purposes in connection with the sale and exploitation of Master and records manufactured from the Master, or to refrain therefrom.

2.   I agree that I will not assert any claim regarding the payment of any advances, fees and/or royalties, as the case may be, against the Artist, the Company or Company's licensees or assigns, or attempt to prevent the manufacture, sale or distribution of records or other uses of the Master. Any payments that I receive from the Artist, the Company or Company's licensees in connection with the exploitation of the Master or my services pursuant to the Producer Agreement shall have been made solely as an accommodation to Company and nothing contained herein, or in the Producer Agreement shall constitute us a beneficiary of or party to any other agreement involving Company.

3.   Acknowledge and agree that the Master embodying the results and proceeds of my services (i) is prepared within the scope of the Company's engagement of my personal services and is a "work made for hire", or (ii) is prepared as part of a long-playing phonograph record (or its substantial equivalent) which constitutes a work Specially ordered by Company for use as a contribution to a collective work and shall be considered a "work made for hire". I further acknowledge that Company is the exclusive owner of copyright with respect to such Master (excluding the copyright to the underlying

Musical composition embodied thereon) and any "sound recording" or "phonorecord" or "copy" manufactured therefrom (individually and collectively called the "Work"), and that Company has the right to exercise all rights of the copyright proprietor with respect thereto, including, but not limited to, all exclusive right specified in 17 U.S.C. 106 and the exclusive right to register copyright in the name of Company.

4.   Agree, notwithstanding the provisions of paragraph above, that to the extent, if any, that I may be deemed "authors" of any Work, I hereby irrevocably transfer, grant, convey and assign to Company, exclusively, perpetually and throughout the universe, all exclusive right, title and interest in and to such Work, including, but not limited to, all exclusive right of the copyright owner as specified in 17 U.S.C. 106. I hereby grant to Company a power of attorney, irrevocable and coupled with an interest, to execute for me and in my name, all documents and instruments necessary or appropriate to effectuate the intents and purposes of this paragraph and to accomplish, evidence and perfect the right granted to Company pursuant to this paragraph including but not limited to documents to apply for and obtain all registration of copyrights in and to any such Work, and documents to assign such copyrights to Company.

5.   Except as specifically set forth in the Producer Agreement to the contrary, agree that I shall not produce or co-produce, prior to the date three (3) years after the Master shall have been delivered to Company in accordance with the provisions of the Agreement, any recording for any person, firm or corporation other than Company which embodies, in whole or in part, any selections recorded in the Master.

Producer:

____

Tony M. Dofat
Dated:

PRODUCER AGREEMENT

25

xxx Records, LLC
xxx Street 20th Floor
New York, NY 10019

Tony M. Dofat
xxxxxxxx
Suite xxx
New York, NY 10036

Dear Producer:

This will confirm the basic terms of the agreement between Producer (the "Producer"), on the one hand, and xxxxx Records LLC ("Company"), on the other hand, concerning Producer's being engaged to produce the artist currently professionally known as "xxxxxx" ("Artist"), as follows:

1.   Company hereby engages the Producer to produce a recording master for the following musical recordings:

Three songs to be determined

The "Master."

2.   The term of this Agreement will commence as of the date hereof and shall continue until the satisfactory completion of the Producers' services hereunder, subject to the ongoing obligations of the parties hereto which survive the expiration of the term hereof. All recording will be at times and places mutually agreed by the parties.

Business and Fundamentals of Music Production

3.	In consideration for the satisfactory completion of all of the Producers' services hereunder and for the rights granted herein, Company has paid the Producer the following compensation:

a.	Advance (i.e., exclusive of all recording costs): ADVANCE AMOUNT Dollars ($15,000) (the "Advance") for the Master as an advance against royalties shall be payable upon the execution hereof. Payment of the Advance and payment of the royalties, (as described below) shall constitute full payment all services rendered by the Producer in connection with the Master, including but not limited to services as a musician, background vocalist or engineer, except as may be separately provided for in a budget approved by the Company in its sole discretion (the "Approved Budget").

b.	With respect to exploitation of the Master or its licensees by means of records, the Company will pay to the Producer a royalty based on net sales of full price albums embodying the Master sold for distribution through normal retail channels in the United States and not returned ("USNRC Net Sales"), determined by multiplying the Royalty Base Price therefore by a royalty rate of Five Percent (5%). The Producer's royalties hereunder shall be pro-rated based on a ratio, the numerator of which is one and the denominator of which is the total number of royalty bearing master recordings on the applicable record, provided that Producer's royalties shall not be pro-rated if the A-Side of a single contains a Master produced by Producer hereunder and the B-Side of such single contains a master not produced by Producers.

c.	With respect to all exploitations of the Master other than in the form of USNRC Net Sales of full-priced albums, the Producer's royalties shall be calculated and adjusted (e.g. subject to the same proportionate deductions and reductions) in the same proportionate manner as Company's corresponding royalties are calculated and adjusted under the Recording Agreement.

d.	With respect to royalties payable under the Recording Agreement which are calculated as a percentage of net

Receipts (e.g. flat fee master use licenses), the Producers' royalty therefor shall be a proportionate share of such net receipts received by or credited to Company computed according to the ratio, which the Producer's royalty rate hereunder bears to Company's basic U.S. royalty rate under the Recording Agreement (the "Producer's Percentage").

e.   In computing royalties hereunder, all relevant terms shall have the same meanings as in the Recording Agreement. No royalty shall be payable to the Producer until such time as all Recording Costs for the Master (as defined in the Recording Agreement, but not including for this purpose any so-called "in pocket" advances paid to Artist, or the Advance) have been recouped at the so-called "net artist rate" (Company's basic royalty rate in the Recording Agreement in respect of the Master, less the Producer's royalty rate for the Master hereunder), at which time the Producer shall receive the Producer's royalties retroactive to the first record sold, subject to deduction of the Advance. Notwithstanding the foregoing to the contrary, Producers' royalty shall not be reduced by the royalty payable to any mixer or re-mixer of the Master or any outside Producer engaged after the Master has been delivered and accepted hereunder.

4.   Except as specifically defined herein, all terms used herein shall have the same meaning as set forth in the Recording Agreement, which is incorporated hereto and may a part hereof.

5.   The Company will account and pay the Producer's royalties not less frequently than semi-annually. Producer shall have the right upon reasonable advance written notice to Company to inspect Company's books and records at Company's normal place of business during normal business hours, as the same may relate specifically to the royalties payable to the Producer hereunder, provided that the Producer shall only have the right to do so With respect to any royalty statement within 2 and one half years of the date such statement was rendered, and only once with respect to any such statement.

6.   If Company receives any monies or is credited with

Any monies against advances previously received from persons or entities other than the Company, including by way of example monies paid by Sound Exchange or AARC ("Defined Third Parties") which are attributable to the exploitation of the Master in connection with either digital performing rights in masters or blank recording media levies (but specifically excluding monies paid to or credited to Company/Artist from the exploitation of the musical composition embodied in the Master) or any other "direct" monies, Producer shall be entitled to an amount equal to a portion of such monies multiplied by a fraction, the numerator of which shall be Producer's royalty rate hereunder and the denominator of which is the "all-in" basic royalty rate payable to Company with respect to the album.

7.   Producer agrees to produce each Master hereunder for the amount specified in the Approved Budget. Producer shall be responsible for any costs incurred in excess of the Approved Budget ("Overages"), unless such Overages were caused by Artist's or Company's decisions or actions or lack thereof. To the extent Company pays any Overages which are Producer's responsibility, Producer agrees that Company may apply any installment of the applicable Advance and any record royalties payable to the Producer hereunder against such repayment obligation.

8.   The Producer agrees to render all services pertaining to the production of the Master, as and when reasonably requested by Company, and as may otherwise be necessary to produce and complete delivery of the fully completed, rough mixed Master, commercially and technically satisfactory to the Company, including but not limited to attending meetings, recording sessions, and all mixing sessions. The Producer shall produce the Master in all respects in accordance with the recording and delivery procedures and

Requirements reasonably requested by Company.

9.   The Producer acknowledges that all performances

Rendered by the Producer or anyone engaged by the Producer which are embodied in the Master will be on a "work-for-hire" basis (as that term is commonly used in the music industry), and that, as between Company and the Producer, the Master shall be the sole and exclusive property of Company free from any claims by the Producers or anyone deriving rights through the Producer, excluding the underlying compositions. If, for any reason, any such performances are not deemed to be work for hire, this Agreement shall operate as an irrevocable assignment of all rights, thereto, to Company and its licensees. The Producer also hereby grant to Company and its licensees the right to use the

10.	Producer's names, as well as approved likenesses and approved biographical data, in connection with the exploitation of the Master and records derived from the Master.

11.	Promptly after the execution hereof, the Producer may provide Company with approved pictures of and biographical material concerning the Producers, which the Producers would like, used in connection with the Master. Company shall have the right to reject said photographs and biographical material only on reasonable grounds. In the event that Company rejects the photographs and/or biographical material provided by the Producer, Company may make available to the Producer for the Producer's approval photographs and biographical material concerning the Producer to be used as set forth in this paragraph. The Producer's approval of said materials shall not be unreasonably withheld and shall be deemed given unless the Producer's disapproval is accompanied by a reasonable reason therefor, and has been received by Company within seven (7) business days after such materials have been made available to the Producer.

12.	The Producer warrants and represents that the Producer

has the authority and power to grant the rights granted herein and that Producer's contributions to the Master will be entirely original, and The use thereof shall not infringe upon the rights of any person, firm or entity. The Producer agree to indemnify and hold Artist and the Company and their respective affiliates and assigns harmless from and against any claims which are inconsistent with the foregoing, or with any representations, obligations or agreements in this Agreement. The foregoing indemnity shall only apply to claims reduced to final, adverse judgment or settled with the Producer's written consent, not to be unreasonably withheld, except for sample claims, if any. Company shall use reasonable efforts to promptly notify the Producer of any claim and Company shall grant the Producer the right to participate in any action at the Producer's sole expense, provided that Company retains the right to control such action. Without limiting the generality of the foregoing, the amount of any monies payable to the Producer hereunder may be reduced by the amount of any liability to which the foregoing indemnity relates. In addition, payment of such monies may be withheld pending the determination of any claim to which the foregoing indemnity relates, provided that the amount so withheld shall not exceed a good faith estimate of the amount of the potential liability involved and will be released (plus interest at the prime rate established by Bank of America) if no formal action is taken with respect to any such claim within 1 year of when the claim was first made, provided that in lieu of any withholding pursuant to this paragraph, Producer shall have the right to make bonding arrangements, satisfactory to Company in its sole discretion to ensure Company of reimbursement for all damages, liabilities, costs and expenses (including reasonable legal fees) which Company or its licensees may occur as a result of any such claim.

13.   The Producer agrees to promptly execute and deliver to Company at Company's sole cost any further documents which Company may reasonably request to evidence or effectuate the provisions hereof.

14.   The Producer agrees not to produce any composition recorded hereunder for any

other person for the purpose of making records for a period of 3 years from the date of delivery of the Master hereunder.

15.   The Producer agrees to be bound by the so-called "controlled composition" provisions in the Recording Agreement, and agree to issue a mechanical license for Producer's share of the Composition in accordance therewith, as well as free synch licenses for any promotional videos embodying the Master.

16.   With respect to the Master produced by the Producer, the Producer shall be entitled to receive appropriate credit as producer of the Master, in substantially the following form: "Produced by Tony Dofat for The TDC Group, Inc." Such credit shall appear in the liner notes, labels and/or back covers of records containing the Master (including in singles derived therefrom if it is then the Company's policy to accord producer credit on singles). Such credit shall also appear in all one-half (1/2) page or larger trade advertisements placed by Company with respect to the Master and/or with respect to records containing the Master if the Master is listed on such advertisement or any producers of such records (other than executive producer credits) are listed on such advertisement (including Billboard strip ads). Notwithstanding the foregoing, no inadvertent failure to provide said credit by Company shall be deemed to be a material breach of this Agreement, provided that if the Producers shall notify Company of such failure, Company shall use reasonable efforts to rectify the failure on a prospective basis.

17.   Company may assign all or part of this Agreement to any entity affiliated with or owned or controlled by the Company, its other distributors or its affiliates or distributors, and any rights so assigned may be similarly assigned by any of the foregoing assignees, provided no such assignment shall relieve Company of its obligations to Producer hereunder, for which Company will remain secondarily responsible. The Producer may not assign any of the Producer's obligations hereunder.

18.   This Agreement is deemed to have been entered into and wholly performed in the State of New York, and its laws shall apply in its interpretation. The New York Courts shall have sole jurisdiction over any action, which either party brings against the other hereunder, and the parties hereby agree that any such action must be brought in New York, New York, and nowhere else. In the event of any action, suit or proceeding by any party hereto against any other party hereto under this Agreement, the prevailing party shall be entitled to recover its attorneys' fees in addition to the cost of said action, suit or proceeding.

19.   This Agreement shall constitute the full and final expression of the agreement of the parties hereto with respect to the production of the Master. All references to "Producer" hereunder shall refer to the above named individual and his loan out and other affiliated companies, individually and jointly. All notices to the Producers or Company shall be sent to the respective addresses first set forth above.

20.   Any so-called "samples" (i.e. third party copyrighted material) which the Producer wishes to incorporate into the Master must be fully disclosed to and approved by Company in advance of any recording thereof. If such sample use is approved, the Producer will not be responsible for any sample clearance fees or royalties payable to the owner of the original master recording unless mutually approved; however, the Producer shall be responsible for any fees or copyright participations to the owners of the underlying musical material. If such sample use is not approved, the Producer will fully indemnify and hold Artist, Company, and their respective licensees harmless from any liability.

Tony M Dofat

If the foregoing reflects the understanding of the parties, please so indicate by signing in the spaces provided for below.

Very truly yours,

XXXXX Records LLC

By: ___________________________________
An Authorized Signatory

AGREED AND ACCEPTED BY:

____

Tony M. Dofat

ATTORNEY RETAINER LETTER

Attorneys At Law

New York, NY 10036
Direct:

July 24, 2012

<u>VIA EMAIL</u>
Mr. Tony Dofat

New York, NY 10016

    Re: ***Retainer Agreement***

Dear Tony:

    This will confirm our agreement as to the terms and conditions under which you have retained this firm to represent your company, LLC ("Company") in connection with all of the Company's entertainment business activities (the "Representation Matters").

    This letter will serve to define the scope of our engagement, confirm that we are in mutual agreement with respect to the work we are expected to perform on your behalf, set forth the financial arrangements pursuant to which we will undertake to represent you, and confirm your approval of all of the arrangements set forth herein. Our duties shall consist of counseling and advice, structuring, negotiating and drafting of agreements and other usual and customary legal services related to the Representation Matters.

    In consideration of the above services, you have agreed to pay this firm a retainer fee ("Retainer Fee") of One Thousand ($1,000.00) Dollars, per month. The Retainer Fee amount shall be subject to change, upon written confirmation of any such agreed upon change by both Company and this firm.

    The Retainer Fee shall be payable by the first day of each month for which services are to be rendered; provided however, that August 2012's Retainer Fee payent shall be made upon execution hereof. Within a reasonable period of time prior to November 1st, 2012, we shall mutually agree upon the Retainer Fee to be paid for November 2012, and thereafter, based upon the Company's development and needs.

    Excluded from the services which are to be rendered by us under this agreement are the following services, should they be required: litigation, corporate, tax, trademark and estate planning and other non-entertainment matters (the "Excluded Services").

    We will provide you with, monthly bills which will provide a breakdown of costs incurred on your behalf during the preceding month. These costs may include, without limitation, copying costs, long distance telephone charges, travel costs, messenger service, Federal Express charges, and the like. We will not incur any substantial costs without first obtaining your prior approval of such expenditure. You agree to pay these statements within fourteen (14) days following your receipt of such statements.

July 24, 2012
Page 2

Please sign and return this letter evidencing your consent and acceptance of the provisions contained herein, together with a wire transfer for the August 2012 Retainer Fee in the amount of One Thousand ($1,000.00) Dollars to the following account:

This agreement shall be terminable by you or this firm, at any time, upon ten (10) days written notice. Following such termination, your obligation to pay this firm for any services rendered hereunder, shall not cease, and you shall be obligated to pay fees and disbursements due and owing in connection with services rendered. **This Retainer Agreement will not take effect and this firm will have no obligation to continue to provide legal services until you sign and return this Retainer Agreement.**

If the foregoing terms and conditions of our engagement are acceptable to you, please signify your approval by signing where indicated and returning the executed letter to us for countersignature.

Very truly yours,

ACCEPTED AND AGREED TO:
I have read and understood the foregoing terms and agree to them, as of the date first provided services on my behalf.

LLC

By: _______________________________
       Tony Dofat

Its: Executive Vice President

Federal ID Number:

Chapter 6

Producer Advance and Royalties

Overview

- How producers get paid
- What are royalties
- Royalty calculations
- What is recoupment

Being a Record producer usually starts off as a hobby or craft until you begin to develop your ear or sound to produce commercial compositions, which could fit in today's marketplace. Once you pass the novice and hobby stage and start generated revenue, you will notice that there are multiple ways to create a more than average income.

Producer Fee (advance)

As a record producer, your compensation is determined by experience and track record. The formula is simple, the bigger your audience, the bigger your producers advance and royalty scale is. When I say audience, I'm referring to radio spins, record sales, chart position, and popularity of your prior releases. Labels tend to hire producers with consistent track records to somewhat assure them of a hit record but this is not always the case.

The standard payment schedule for producers is usually received in 50% prior to any work being done and the remaining 50% backend or balance is paid out once the record label accepts your master. You will be required to sign several short contracts with the record company per master or project. The two initial contracts consist of a producer's declaration and a deal memo or short form agreement as mentioned .in the previous chapter. Once the master is recorded,

Delivered, and accepted, you will be presented a long form agreement outlining every minor detail in conjunction with your delivered Masters including liner notes credit, use of name, recoupment, term, territory, etc. If you have numerous hits within the top 5 or 10 on Billboard then your fee should definitely be more than, let's say a person that have not charted at all. Your sound is more popular than the producer that has not yet charted which would equate to more radio spins and club play, not to say that his material is sub par but this is considered earning your stripes in this biz and sometimes the label will use this to their advantage to pay the new producer scraps of a budget. Regardless of your fee amount, it is 100% recoupable against your future royalties.

The producer fee is payment for your time, resources, your unique sound, and your ability to deliver a great quality song, keep in mind that this figure is always negotiable. Please don't get caught in a situation where you may receive a huge check and the label may state that you won't have to pay it back but it will show on your royalty statement as an advance, and advances are always recoupable. The ONLY monies that are non-recoupable are "Bonuses". Bonuses usually happen when you sell gold status (500,000 units) or platinum (1,000,000 units). Bonuses can also happen upon signing if you were part of a bidding war, labels usually likes to throw bonuses to persuade the artist to sign with them, Often times, they may entice them with Rolexes, cars, material items, or even production imprint deals.

The producer fees for a middle tier producer in the mid 90's was an estimated $7,500-$10,000. If you are a top 10 producer on the chart, you will possibly receive somewhere in the neighborhood of $25,000 fee. I know producers that have received as much as $250,000 advance for just 1 song. My 1st song Puffy and I produced; we received only $3,500 in which we had to split. The producer fee is just 1 stream of revenue received by the producer, another huge stream is the producer mechanical royalty.

Producer Royalty

A producer royalty is a percentage of each album sold in any format. Yes, producers are entitled to a royalty but all producers receive different percentages. This again depends on your track record, popularity, and how much will you contribute to the sale of the album. New producers start out at a standard 3 points. As you begin to build a nice resume or discography, your point structure will gradually increase to 3.5 points then to 4 points. I have received as much as 5 points throughout my career. What is a point? To break is down, labels have to recoup all expenses to produce, duplicate, promote, market, Etc. Once the label recoups (usually around 250k - 500k sales) there is a formula to compensate everyone that has been awarded a royalty pursuant to their deal memo or contract. Labels use a point system because it unknown to put a dollar value on a point until you calculate by using the formula (see below).

Although this is not considered publishing money, I'm going to include here an explanation of retail royalties. They are often confused with publishing because the money an artist receives is called a "royalty." This is one of the main areas of negotiation in a recording contract. These royalties, also known as "points" are based on a percentage of the manufacturer's suggested retail selling price for every unit sold AFTER the artist recoups. "Recoup" means to pay back most of the money spent on the project such as advances, recording, usually half the video costs, and often half of the independent radio budget. Most recording contracts specify what is recoupable and what is not (another area of negotiation is to reduce the recoupable items and to set limits on what can be spent in areas such as video, radio promotions, free goods, etc.).

Royalty Calculation

Retail Royalties usually run between 11 points and 18 points (a point is roughly equal to 8 cents per unit sold). And in the true fashion of a record label reducing what they have to pay the artist

Whenever they get the chance, some contracts include "packaging deductions," special "CD rates," and/or "breakage fees" to further reduce the royalty. There is always a reduction in points for units sold outside of the United States (US and Canada should almost always be paid at 100%, and I'd even try to negotiate to include all of North America if I were doing the deal) as well. The more leverage an artist has in the negotiations, the higher the point structure usually. If the artist has a strong buzz or has sold a lot of units prior to being signed, it should not be difficult to secure 18 points. But again, points, or retail record royalties are only paid after an artist recoups, so if too much money is spent on marketing the project, videos are shot for hundreds of thousands of dollars, and the artist is unrecouped, it doesn't matter how many points are involved--it could be 100, no money will be paid to the artist. Almost all artists are unrecouped which also refers to the term "In the red". Most artists' never make free from the red zone, which could be a major hardship while trying to raise a family. You, as the artist must generate multiple revenue streams (Live Shows, Merchandise, Endorsement Deals, Appearances) to stay afloat.

Chapter 7

Songwriting

Overview

> • What is a songwriter
> • Methods of songwriting
> • Dealing with creative blocks
> • Lyric and music writing guide

As a great songwriter, you must relive certain scenarios and explain it in a song format along with a melody in such a way, it can be emotionally felt and accepted by your audience. As an artist, you must play the role of an actor and put yourself in the shoes of writer to express and relay the message to your fans by sounding convincing and believable.

Writing may flow easier for some than others because of their life experiences. Traveling, partying, your community or surroundings, nightclub atmosphere, etc. will play an important role in your songwriting. It is pretty difficult to give a full detailed description about a person, place or thing if you have not experienced or seen it through your own eyes. Your audience will be able to distinguish the difference between a person, which have not experienced much to those who have travelled the world with an abundance of life experiences.
For example; try writing a song after a certain major life experience such as a relationship break-up and watch the difference and your choice of words. Lyrically, a song shouldn't take a long time to write (maybe a few hours). It should come together organically and just flow like water. Most times, your initial thoughts or feelings are usually the best and may need a bit of tweaking later but this is a natural process. Overthinking creativity can sometimes ruin a hit in the

Making and also be careful not to have to many cooks in the kitchen, this will distract you even more. I usually suggest and recommend writers to vibe and hang around other writers, producers to gel with other producers, and so on and so forth. This will allow you to see how others create and formulate their magic, which could enhance your area of creativity.

Sometimes while writing, you may get stuck trying to pen your words; this is referred to as a "writer's block". This is a common occurrence and has happened to the best of the best. Why does our creativity get blocked? Stress, tension, overthinking, and simple distractions are some of the obvious reasons for writer's block but can be easily fixed by changing your environment or stimulating certain senses. Stimulating senses such as lighting or lighting color, wall treatment color, scented candles and aromas, the presence of particular people can also offset your creativity. If you've ever visited a recording studio, notice the colors patterns surrounding the studio walls, and the lighting. This purpose is to create a productive working mood and is used to assist in transferring our thoughts into art. Changing your environment may help by seeing a particular action or thing, which could inspire or spark your imagination. I can recall on numerous occasions where I would leave the studio [or wherever I was creating] completely and go for a walk just to change my surroundings. Sometimes I would return maybe 30 minutes to an hour later with a totally different outlook on my composition.

The song concept can be anything that your heart and mind is feeling at that particular moment. Remember, music is art and art is your interpretation and expression by using your human creative skills and imagination. Concept is your song blueprint and foundation and is a very key element as with building a house or structure. This process of record making is referred to painting the picture. Conceptually, an easy way to penning a hit song is talking about something that the masses can relate to in their every day living yet maintaining a commercially satisfactory feel. Love, Relationships, heartbreaks,

Attraction is usually a standard lyric concept of the majority of hits and has worked fine for decades. Everyone can relate to love, relationships, and break-ups.

A great way to watch your concept bloom into a great song is by charting the stages of your vision by using either the alphabet (A to Z) or numbers (1-10). For example; the letter "Z" will be your finish point and the last stop of your vision, the letter "A" will be your start point. Every stage of your production must follow in line with your concept. There are several ways to write a full composition consisting of words and music. Every producer and composer has their own way of completing this; there is no wrong or right way, as long as the final product is along the lines of your expectations.

I created flow chart examples for 3 different methods to writing full compositions from inception to consumer; this is a great guide and is very useful for the beginner. These 3 examples can work with all live instrumentation, if you're using a DAW, or if you're combining live instruments with your DAW.

- **EXAMPLE 1**

This songwriting example is the base for writing Hip-Hop music. Normally, the producer would build the sequence or music with drums or a drum loop. After the drum loop is sequenced, you will determine the tempo by truncating or adjusting the start and end points to the loop. Next, the keyboards or music samples are added, doing this step would finalize the key of the song. I would normally add more drums after this stage, high hats, shakers, and percussion.

- **EXAMPLE 2**

This songwriting example is the base for writing music around the lyrics and vocals. The first stage is determining the tempo by tapping or by using a metronome. Next, the writer of the words creates the melody and lyrics. We would usually record a rough reference track of this so the composers of the music can vibe to the vocalist's melody with a keyboard or instrument. Once the producer determines the chord structure, this is sequenced or recorded. Now is the time to start your full song arrangement, which would put you at the halfway point of this method. After the arrangement is complete, the composer or programmer would add the drum track and you would continue to finish the song as described in the flow chart.

- **EXAMPLE 3**

This songwriting example is the base for writing music traditionally either live or using your DAW. The tempo is determined first then the key of the song is next. The song key is usually at the top of the flow charts because this will determine the feel of your composition. Next, the musician or composer would find a great melody, either by humming it or playing it on an instrument. Once the melody is locked in, drums are usually added at this point. Some songs may not have drums but this is totally up to the producer. After the drums are added, percussion would follow. The arrangement stage is usually mid-way to completion; this is done after you're satisfied with the sounds and feel of your composition thus far. Bass can then be added, some songs only have bass lines in the chorus or hook sections so this is once again the producer's decision. The composition will continue

To gradually build as described in the flow chart until the final stage, which is the mastering step.

EXAMPLE 1

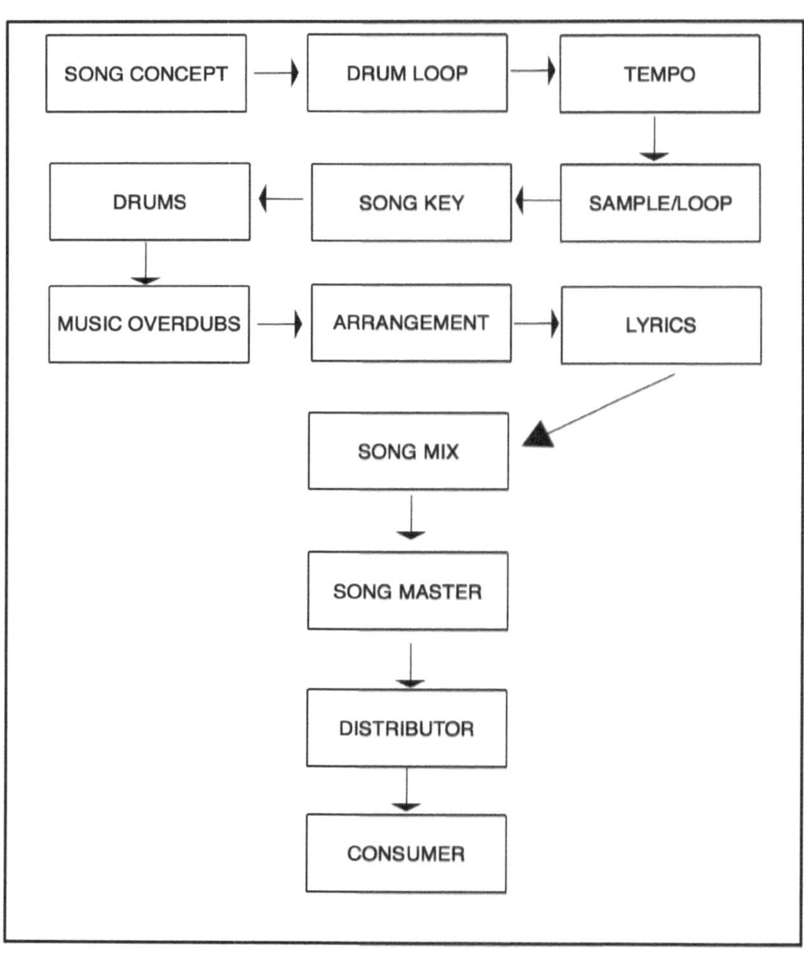

EXAMPLE 2

SONG CONCEPT
TEMPO
LYRIC MELODY
ARRANGEMENT
MUSIC / CHORDS
SONG KEY
DRUMS
MUSIC OVERDUBS
VOCAL OVERDUBS
SONG MIX
SONG MASTER
DISTRIBUTOR
CONSUMER

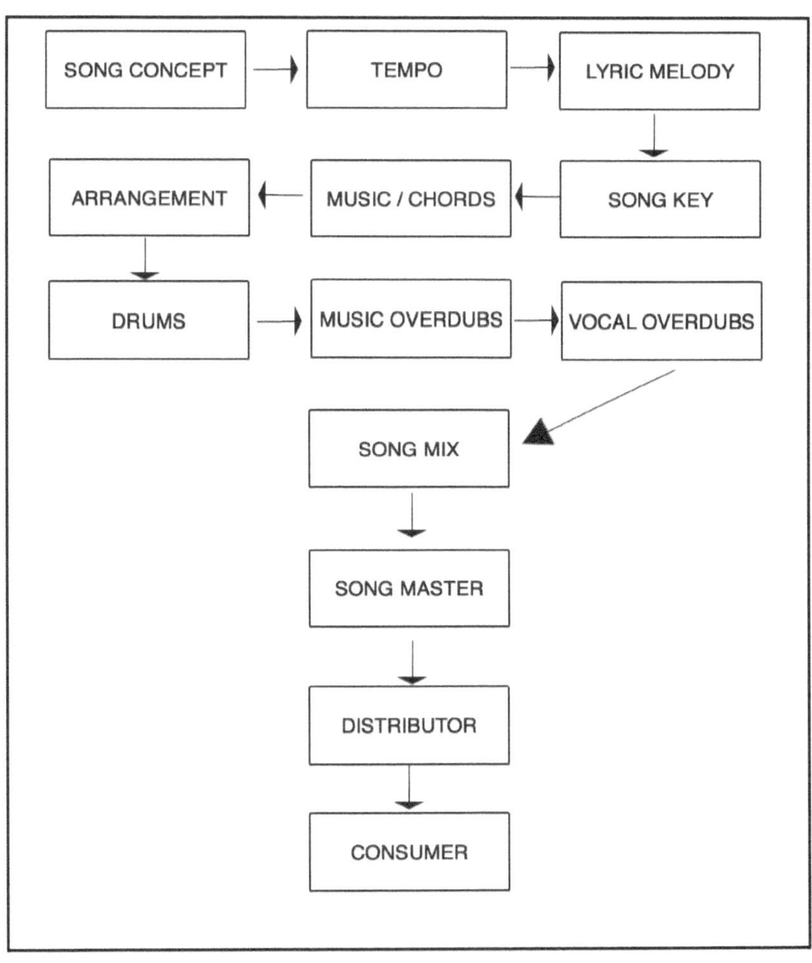

EXAMPLE 3

SONG CONCEPT
TEMPO
SONG KEY
PERCUSSION
DRUMS
SONG MELODY
ARRANGEMENT
BASS
MUSIC OVERDUBS
SONG MIX
LYRICS
VOCAL MELODY
SONG MASTER
DISTRIBUTOR
CONSUMER

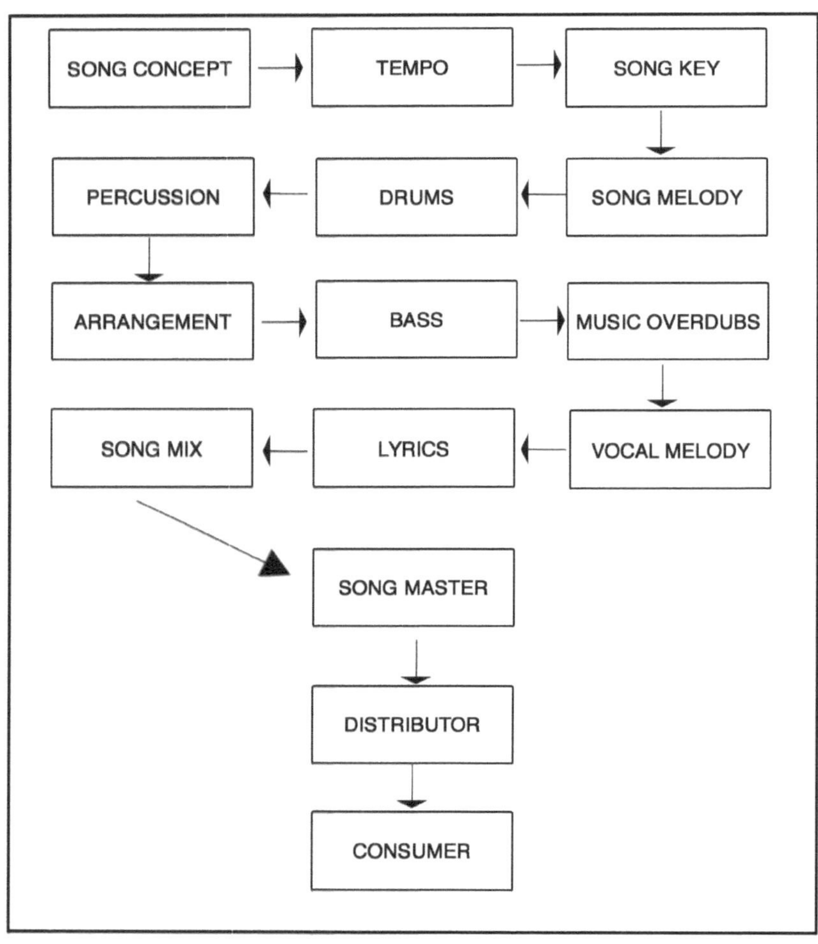

Chapter 8

The Remix

There are a few different variations to the meaning of a remix. In the EDM or dance world, a remix is different than the Reggae or dance hall genre and the same with urban music. The simplest way to define a remix is it's an alternate version of a composition by editing and using the vocal tracks and creating new music for a specific genre. For example; if you have an urban top 10 hit, the label or manager would request a remix to be done for the particular song so it would allow the composition to cross barriers into a different genre to gain a larger audience. The label would usually do a dance version, an EDM version, or a hip-hop version to capture all audiences. Remixes are also created and promoted to lengthen the life span of a song during a promotional campaign meaning that if you're tired of the old version, a new version or "remix" would be introduced to the fans and audience which could sometimes encourage the radio to continue to play the song for 3 to 6 months longer. Remixes and alternate versions count as a detection with media base and BDS which is helpful while trying to break a new artist or song. It would appear that the original song is getting massive airplay, meanwhile it's the remix that is getting all of the spins. Remixes are rarely done for monetary purposes but are used to generate more sales of an album or sales of the original single. The remixers or Producers of the remix usually gets paid a flat fee without any mechanical

Royalties or publishing, even if the music is totally different or a new composition is derived.

Remixes started in the 70's with reggae and dub genres, producers like King Tubby and Lee Perry would strip down their masters and begin to make alternate versions which became Very popular. Most times, they would add delays or echos on vocal snippets to create something new.

On the pop side, artist's like Madonna and other huge disco or dance artists during the 80's began doing edits to their original masters to lengthen them for club use, these versions were called dub mixes, club mixes, or extended versions. They would take a 4-minute song and edit it to make it a 10 or sometimes 15-minute version with various beat drops and vocal edits which did make the song more appealing to the nightclub goers.

Not until the 90's when Diddy and myself would embark on the idea of making a totally new composition and sometimes even recut new vocal performances to start the trend of the urban remix. The urban remixes started in the early 90's with the support of Andre Harrell's Uptown Records/MCA, which is now Universal Music Group. We were the first producers to fully Master the art of remixing with artists such as Mary J Blige, Jodeci, and Christopher Williams. The remix was rather successful and changed the sound of urban music forever.

Most times when you hear a song on the radio or watch the video, there's a 50% chance that these versions may be the remix or alternate mix version and not the original. This would Confuse the consumer would fool them into buying an album which did not contain what was heard on the radio or video; however, this was during the pre-digital era. Now you can preview songs prior to purchasing them. Sometimes, remixes are rolled out before the main version and with some cases; the original main version may not be released at all for several reasons. Urban music changes rather quickly (maybe every 3 months) because the hip-hop culture is a fast changing lifestyle. If an

Artist takes a long time to record their album, the original song could be out dated but could still be a great composition with potential so the Executive Producer or label A&R would call for a remix budget and hire a top remixer or producer to remix the song in hopes to salvage what is remaining.

Depending on your track record, there have been some cases where the producer or composer of the remix is awarded mechanical and publishing. There was great support for this argument. Imagine, a song being remixed and then topped the charts to platinum status and the original writers and producers would fully benefit from the re-mixed version and the remixer gets nothing but a work for hire fee. I have received publishing and mechanical royalties from remixes plenty of times. Technically, remixes are done by creating a tempo map around the acapella track and if you're asked to do a Hip-Hop remix then loops or drums would be added to the vocal tracks. A lot of DJ's are responsible for some huge remixes because the DJ's are the first to collect the acapella versions from the labels and then make their own blends for club play or mix tapes. Sometimes songs are considered remixes if the artist decides to add a side artist or a guest feature appearance on the song but the music will stays as the original master. The output rate of remixes have declined after the early to mid 2000, artists would just scrap a song if it wasn't good or they would toss it on a mix tape and give it away for free.

Chapter 9

Publishing, Copyright, and Sampling

Overview

- What is publishing
- The purpose of a publisher
- What is sampling and interpolation
- Forms associated with sampling
- What is a copyright

As a songwriter or producer, you may often collaborate and co-write with someone else. When this happens, you must make sure that all of your split-sheets and copyright forms are filled out accurately or if there are disputes, the performance right organizations will not pay anyone until the dispute is settled. Each song should total 100%; the breakdown is 50% for the lyric and melody, the remaining 50% for the composer of the music. There is a method most writers use to calculate percentages of publishing and writer's share per contribution below.

This pertains to the words and melody portion and should equal to 50%.

Hook = 20%
Verse = 10% each (2 verses would equal 20%)
Bridge=10%

This method has worked fine for decades but as long as all parties agree, you can distribute any amounts of percentages, as you like. Let's compare these percentages to equity, which is owned and controlled by you, the writer. Every time the song plays via radio,

Streaming services, Etc. your composition will accrue revenue, which we refer to as "pipeline".

There are several types of royalties but this specific royalty is called your "Performance Royalty and is paid out via your performance rights organization (PRO). Another type of royalties are "Mechanical royalties" which derives from record sales and the record label pay these. There are also "Synchronization royalties" which is a royalty paid out for use in film or television. This is where your publisher or publishing company gets involved.

Your publisher, which most times are you (self published) role is to collect the funds according to your percentage. You can assign a larger publishing company such as Warner Chappell, Universal, Sony ATV, Etc. to administer your publishing catalog for a minimal fee. If there is a publishing percentage dispute, all payments are withheld until all parties involved come to an agreement, thus the importance for split sheets upon creating the composition. Publishing is probably the most lucrative revenue stream in the music business, as long as you maintain your copyright percentage, the revenue will continue to flow. Let us discuss copyright protection in this next section.

When dealing with copyright forms, there are 2 forms pertinent to music, the descriptions and forms are as followed;

When to Use Form SR (Sound Recordings)

Use Form SR for registration of published or unpublished sound recordings, that is, for registration of the particular sounds or recorded performance. Form SR must also be used if you wish to make one registration for both the sound recording and the underlying work (the musical composition, dramatic, or literary work). You may make a single registration only if the copyright claimant is the same for both the sound recording and the underlying work. In this case, the

Authorship statement in Space 2 should specify that the claim covers both works.

Form SR is also the appropriate form for registration of a multimedia kit that combines two or more kinds of authorship including a sound recording (such as a kit containing a book and an audiocassette).

When to Use Form PA (Performing Arts)

For registration purposes, musical compositions and dramatic works that are recorded on disks or cassettes are works of the performing arts and should be registered on Form PA or Short Form PA. Therefore, if you wish to register only the underlying work that is a musical composition or dramatic work, use Form PA even though you may send a disk or cassette.

Online Registration

Online registration through the electronic Copyright Office (eCO) is the preferred way to register basic claims. Advantages of online filing include

- A lower filing fee
- Fastest processing time
- Online status tracking
- Secure payment by credit or debit card, electronic check, or Copyright Office deposit account
- The ability to upload certain categories of deposits directly into eCO as electronic files note: You can still register using eCO and save money even if you will submit a hard-copy deposit. The system will prompt you to specify whether you intend to submit an electronic or a hard-copy deposit, and it will provide instructions accordingly. Hard-copy deposits are required for published works. Basic claims include (1) a single work; (2) multiple unpublished works if the

Elements are assembled in an orderly form; the combined elements bear a single title identifying the collection as a whole; the copyright claimant in all the Elements and in the collection as a whole is the same; and all the elements are by the same author, or, if they are by different authors, at least one of the authors has Contributed copyrightable authorship to each element; and (3) multiple published works if they are all first published together in the same publication on the same date and owned by the same claimant. To register online, go to the Copyright Office website at www.copyright.gov and click on electronic Copyright Office.

Registration with Paper Forms

- Paper versions of Form PA (performing arts works, including motion pictures) and Form SR (sound recordings) are available on the Copyright Office website. Staff will send them to you by postal mail upon request. Remember that online registration through eCO can be used for these types of applications.

Mailing Addresses for Applications Filed on Paper and for Hard-Copy Deposits:

Library of Congress U.S. Copyright Office
101 Independence Avenue SE
Washington, DC 20559

- Note: Copyright office fees are subject to change. For current fees, please check the Copyright office website at www.copyright.gov, write the Copyright office, or call (202) 707-3000.

- Note: To make a single registration, copyright ownership in the musical composition and in the sound recording must be the same.
- Note: Phonorecords (tapes, cassette tapes, cartridges, discs) are not sound recordings. Phonorecords are physical objects in which various kinds of works can Be fixed. The works them- selves may be musical compositions, literary works, dramatic works, or sound recordings.

Effective Date of Registration

When the Copyright Office issues a registration certificate, it assigns as the effective date of registration the date it received all required elements an application, a nonrefundable filing fee, and a nonreturnable deposit in acceptable form, regardless of how long it took to process the application and mail the certificate. You do not have to receive your certificate before you publish or produce your work, nor do you need permission from the Copyright Office to place a copyright notice on your work. However, the Copyright Office must have acted on your application before you can file a suit for copyright infringement, and certain remedies, such as statutory damages and attorney's fees, are available only for acts of infringement that occurred after the effective date of registration. If a published work was infringed before the effective date of registration, those remedies may also be available if the effective date of registration is no later than 90 days after the first publication of the work.

If you apply online for copyright registration, you will receive an email saying that your application was received.

If you apply for copyright registration using a paper application, you will not receive an acknowledgment that your application has been received (the Office receives more than 600,000 applications annually), but you can expect:

- A letter or a telephone call from a Copyright Office staff member if further information is needed or

- A certificate of registration indicating that the work has been registered, or if the application cannot be accepted, a letter explaining why it has been rejected Requests to have certificates available for pickup in the Copyright Office or to have certificates sent by Federal Express or another mail service cannot be honored.

Sample and Interpolation

60's and 70's artists have been sampled since the beginning of Hip-Hop, 90's artists sample a lot of 80's artists, and so on but sample laws did not take full effect until the late 80's because sampling was a new technology. Sampling is when composer or producer records music snippets or sounds into a sampler from a pre existing song, usually from a CD or vinyl. Producers would sample and loop beats or breaks, 1 to 2 bars, sometimes 4 or 8 bars with the purpose of creating a new composition. This was the foundation and backbone of hip-hop since it's inception, the only difference was DJ's would mix the break beats live with 2 turntables and a mixer. After artist's sampled material, an artist would rap or sing over the new composition and then commercially release the material without any repercussions until the labels, publishers, and the sampled artists got fed up with people ripping off their property. Some of the derivative work would sell a lot of units but unfortunately, the original composers and master owners would not receive compensation or credit for contributing to the new composition derived from their work. After the sample laws became fully enforced in the late 80's, anything containing a sample must be granted a license for usage by the publisher and master owner. Publishers and record labels would begin receiving advances, publishing share in the new composition, and writer's credit. The amount of advance and publishing share varied, depended upon the discretion of the publisher and record label.

For starters, an average quote would range from a $5,000 to $25,000 advance for the master license, 25% to 50% publishing share of the new composition, as well as a mechanical and performance royalty. To clear new compositions containing samples, you would hire a Sample Clearance Company and submit information along with the original song as well as the new composition. When hiring the sample clearance company, they would request to grant usage from the owners of the sampled song and negotiate the terms on your behalf, both master and publishing usage. If you lift any audio from the actual vinyl, cassette, or CD from any pre existing material, this would be considered a master usage and must be cleared in conjunction as with the writers of that material which is the publishing side of the song. In some cases, artists and/or labels would deny usage to the new compositions if it's too vulgar or if it represents the artist or original song in a distasteful manner. Prince and Steve Miller are artist's that don't believe in sampling and will not clear usage of any type, regardless of any monetary offer. Sampling has allowed this new generation to introduce and incorporate music from 20 years ago and make it popular and most times better than the original song.

Interpolation is different from sampling because you're not actually recording music from a pre existing composition but you would replay or recreate parts of the music by musicians or the composer in a DAW. By doing this, you will not have to deal with a master clearance because only the writers portion of the song is being used. This also applies to new composition that use pre existing melodies but use different words or vice versa. Clearance must be approved or you would be considered infringing upon another writer's copyright, which would initiate a lawsuit. (See chapter 10) Interpolations became a huge thing in the mid 90's when the Labels started demanding astronomical fees for sample usage so our cost effective alternative was to replay the sample and add a little extra. This method wiped out the master usage advance, master usage royalty, and most of the time, the new composition sonically and creatively sounded better than the original song.

I produced a Heavy-D song in 1994 called "Who's the man" and it contained less than 2 seconds of Steve Miller's "Fly Like An Eagle". Heavy D reached out to Steve Miller and asked for a courtesy; Steve said he was a fan of Heavy-D so he cleared the sample but under one Condition, he wanted to maintain 100% of the new copyright. I felt it was robbery but at the same time, Mr. Miller denies any sample requests, which made this a bittersweet moment. Heavy agreed to relinquish every percent of our new composition for a 1 second sample. Serendipitously, The song later became Heavy-D's first single from the classic, RIAA certified gold album "Blue Funk." Creatively, a nice piece of work but in my opinion, the 1-second sample would have disappeared if the choice were solely mine.

The following is an actual sample and interpolation form to be filled out by the record producer or by A&R administration department of a record label. Once your sample sheet is filled out, you would submit this to a sample clearance company such as DMG Clearances, Inc. to obtain a license for usage.

WRITER SPLIT SHEET

THE TDC GROUP, INC
Composer/Writer Split Sheets

Song Title:
Recording Artist:
Record Label:

Composer/Writer 1:
Address:

Phone:

Publishing Company:

Publishing %:

Affiliation: ASCAP   BMI   SESAC   (Circle one)

Ownership %:   _________   _________

CAE/Social Security #:
Birthdate:

Writer/Composer Signature _______________**Date:** __________________

Composer/Writer 2:
Address:

Phone:

Publishing Company:

Publishing %:

Affiliation: ASCAP   BMI   SESAC   (Circle one)

Ownership %:   _________   _________

CAE/Social Security #:
Birthdate:

Writer/Composer Signature _______________**Date:** __________________

SAMPLE AND INTERPOLATION FORM

THE TDC GROUP, INC

Sample and Interpolation form

New Song Title:

Recording Artist:

Record Label:

Sample Information:

Artist: ____

Album: ____

Song Title: ____

Writer(s): ____

Publisher(s): ____

Label: ____

Address: ____

Usage (describe): _______________________________________

New Song Information:

Producer(s): ____

Writer(s): ____

Publisher(s): ____

Song Length: ____

Release Date: ____

Album: ____

COPYRIGHT FORM PA

Privacy Act Notice: Sections 408-410 of title 17 of the *United States Code* authorize the Copyright Office to collect the personally identifying information requested on this form in order to process the application for copyright registration. By providing this information you are agreeing to routine uses of the information that include publication to give legal notice of your copyright claim as required by 17 U.S.C. §705. It will appear in the Office's online catalog. If you do not provide the information requested, registration may be refused or delayed, and you may not be entitled to certain relief, remedies, and benefits under the copyright law.

Form PA
For a Work of Performing Arts
UNITED STATES COPYRIGHT OFFICE

REGISTRATION NUMBER

PA   PAU

EFFECTIVE DATE OF REGISTRATION

Month   Day   Year

DO NOT WRITE ABOVE THIS LINE. IF YOU NEED MORE SPACE, USE A SEPARATE CONTINUATION SHEET.

1   TITLE OF THIS WORK ▼

PREVIOUS OR ALTERNATIVE TITLES ▼

NATURE OF THIS WORK ▼ See instructions

2   **a**   NAME OF AUTHOR ▼

DATES OF BIRTH AND DEATH
Year Born ▼   Year Died ▼

Was this contribution to the work a "work made for hire"?
❑ Yes
❑ No

AUTHOR'S NATIONALITY OR DOMICILE
Name of Country
OR { Citizen of ______
Domiciled in ______

WAS THIS AUTHOR'S CONTRIBUTION TO THE WORK
Anonymous? ❑ Yes ❑ No
Pseudonymous? ❑ Yes ❑ No
If the answer to either of these questions is "Yes," see detailed instructions.

NATURE OF AUTHORSHIP Briefly describe nature of material created by this author in which copyright is claimed. ▼

NOTE
Under the law, the "author" of a "work made for hire" is generally the employer, not the employee (see instructions). For any part of this work that was "made for hire" check "Yes" in the space provided, give the employer (or other person for whom the work was prepared) as "Author" of that part, and leave the space for dates of birth and death blank.

b   NAME OF AUTHOR ▼

DATES OF BIRTH AND DEATH
Year Born ▼   Year Died ▼

Was this contribution to the work a "work made for hire"?
❑ Yes
❑ No

AUTHOR'S NATIONALITY OR DOMICILE
Name of Country
OR { Citizen of ______
Domiciled in ______

WAS THIS AUTHOR'S CONTRIBUTION TO THE WORK
Anonymous? ❑ Yes ❑ No
Pseudonymous? ❑ Yes ❑ No
If the answer to either of these questions is "Yes," see detailed instructions.

NATURE OF AUTHORSHIP Briefly describe nature of material created by this author in which copyright is claimed. ▼

c   NAME OF AUTHOR ▼

DATES OF BIRTH AND DEATH
Year Born ▼   Year Died ▼

Was this contribution to the work a "work made for hire"?
❑ Yes
❑ No

AUTHOR'S NATIONALITY OR DOMICILE
Name of Country
OR { Citizen of ______
Domiciled in ______

WAS THIS AUTHOR'S CONTRIBUTION TO THE WORK
Anonymous? ❑ Yes ❑ No
Pseudonymous? ❑ Yes ❑ No
If the answer to either of these questions is "Yes," see detailed instructions.

NATURE OF AUTHORSHIP Briefly describe nature of material created by this author in which copyright is claimed. ▼

3   **a**   YEAR IN WHICH CREATION OF THIS WORK WAS COMPLETED This information must be given in all cases. ______ Year

b   DATE AND NATION OF FIRST PUBLICATION OF THIS PARTICULAR WORK Complete this information ONLY if this work has been published. Month ______ Day ______ Year ______ Nation

4   COPYRIGHT CLAIMANT(S) Name and address must be given even if the claimant is the same as the author given in space 2. ▼

See instructions before completing this space

TRANSFER If the claimant(s) named here in space 4 is (are) different from the author(s) named in space 2, give a brief statement of how the claimant(s) obtained ownership of the copyright. ▼

DO NOT WRITE HERE
OFFICE USE ONLY

APPLICATION RECEIVED

ONE DEPOSIT RECEIVED

TWO DEPOSITS RECEIVED

FUNDS RECEIVED

MORE ON BACK ▶ • Complete all applicable spaces (numbers 5-9) on the reverse side of this page.
• See detailed instructions.   • Sign the form at line 8.

DO NOT WRITE HERE
Page 1 of ______ pages

COPYRIGHT FORM SR

Copyright Office fees are subject to change. For current fees, check the Copyright Office website at www.copyright.gov, write the Copyright Office, or call (202) 707-3000.

Form SR
For a Sound Recording
UNITED STATES COPYRIGHT OFFICE

REGISTRATION NUMBER

SR   SRU

EFFECTIVE DATE OF REGISTRATION

Month   Day   Year

Privacy Act Notice: Sections 408-410 of title 17 of the *United States Code* authorize the Copyright Office to collect the personally identifying information requested on this form in order to process the application for copyright registration. By providing this information you are agreeing to routine uses of the information that include publication to give legal notice of your copyright claim as required by 17 U.S.C. §705. It will appear in the Office's online catalog. If you do not provide the information requested, registration may be refused or delayed, and you may not be entitled to certain relief, remedies, and benefits under the copyright law.

DO NOT WRITE ABOVE THIS LINE. IF YOU NEED MORE SPACE, USE A SEPARATE CONTINUATION SHEET.

1

TITLE OF THIS WORK ▼

PREVIOUS, ALTERNATIVE, OR CONTENTS TITLES (CIRCLE ONE) ▼

2

a

NAME OF AUTHOR ▼

DATES OF BIRTH AND DEATH
Year Born ▼   Year Died ▼

Was this contribution to the work a "work made for hire"?
❑ Yes
❑ No

AUTHOR'S NATIONALITY OR DOMICILE
Name of Country
OR { Citizen of ▶ _______
Domiciled in ▶ _______

WAS THIS AUTHOR'S CONTRIBUTION TO THE WORK
Anonymous?   ❑ Yes ❑ No
Pseudonymous? ❑ Yes ❑ No

If the answer to either of these questions is "Yes," see detailed instructions.

NATURE OF AUTHORSHIP Briefly describe nature of material created by this author in which copyright is claimed. ▼

NOTE

Under the law, the "author" of a "work made for hire" is generally the employer, not the employee (see instructions). For any part of this work that was "made for hire," check "Yes" in the space provided, give the employer (or other person for whom the work was prepared) as "Author" of that part, and leave the space for dates of birth and death blank.

b

NAME OF AUTHOR ▼

DATES OF BIRTH AND DEATH
Year Born ▼   Year Died ▼

Was this contribution to the work a "work made for hire"?
❑ Yes
❑ No

AUTHOR'S NATIONALITY OR DOMICILE
Name of Country
OR { Citizen of ▶ _______
Domiciled in ▶ _______

WAS THIS AUTHOR'S CONTRIBUTION TO THE WORK
Anonymous?   ❑ Yes ❑ No
Pseudonymous? ❑ Yes ❑ No

If the answer to either of these questions is "Yes," see detailed instructions.

NATURE OF AUTHORSHIP Briefly describe nature of material created by this author in which copyright is claimed. ▼

c

NAME OF AUTHOR ▼

DATES OF BIRTH AND DEATH
Year Born ▼   Year Died ▼

Was this contribution to the work a "work made for hire"?
❑ Yes
❑ No

AUTHOR'S NATIONALITY OR DOMICILE
Name of Country
OR { Citizen of ▶ _______
Domiciled in ▶ _______

WAS THIS AUTHOR'S CONTRIBUTION TO THE WORK
Anonymous?   ❑ Yes ❑ No
Pseudonymous? ❑ Yes ❑ No

If the answer to either of these questions is "Yes," see detailed instructions.

NATURE OF AUTHORSHIP Briefly describe nature of material created by this author in which copyright is claimed. ▼

3

a YEAR IN WHICH CREATION OF THIS WORK WAS COMPLETED
This information must be given in all cases.
Year ▶ _______

b DATE AND NATION OF FIRST PUBLICATION OF THIS PARTICULAR WORK
Complete this information ONLY if this work has been published.
Month ▶ _______ Day ▶ _______ Year ▶ _______
Nation ▶ _______

4

a COPYRIGHT CLAIMANT(S) Name and address must be given even if the claimant is the same as the author given in space 2. ▼

See instructions before completing this space

b TRANSFER If the claimant(s) named here in space 4 is (are) different from the author(s) named in space 2, give a brief statement of how the claimant(s) obtained ownership of the copyright. ▼

APPLICATION RECEIVED

ONE DEPOSIT RECEIVED

TWO DEPOSITS RECEIVED

FUNDS RECEIVED

DO NOT WRITE HERE OFFICE USE ONLY

MORE ON BACK ▶ • Complete all applicable spaces (numbers 5-9) on the reverse side of this page.
• See detailed instructions.   • Sign the form at line 8.

DO NOT WRITE HERE
Page 1 of _______ pages

Chapter 10

Becoming a Music Producer

Overview

> - What makes a great music producer
> - Understanding the tools of a producer
> - The differences between producers
> - Getting hired as a producer

As with any skill or profession, there are many tiers to a craft, such as novice or beginner to experienced or expert. Everyone, besides a few genius exceptions, starts as a novice and learn to perfect and hone their craft through hobby experience, interning, formal training, or reading. You may study 10 years to learn the ropes of a music producer but still may not be or become successful as a producer. But why?

There are multiple reasons why many may not overcome the novice or mediocre barrier. The most important thing a lot of entry-level producers do not understand is "music is art" and one who creates music is also considered an "artist." What is art? Art is solely using your imagination and creativity to communicate your emotions by visual or auditory forms. Young and emerging producers do not understand this but once digested, you will see creative doors opening one after another and your wheels will turn continuously. Secondly, just like anything else, music must be one of your high priority passions. Lacking passion will allow your music or "art" to suffer. Money, cars, or material things should not be your motive to write music or spend 18 hours straight in the studio with expectations of releasing an album to become the next microwaveable millionaire. Anything worth having is worth working hard for and anything you

Want is attainable by hard work and passion. All successful music producers have these qualities plus more.

Next, you must develop your main producer's tool, your ear. You must know what commercial music sounds like. One test is to break down one of your favorite song to see why is it your favorite song and how did it become your favorite song. Understand the patterns; drum kits, and sounds as well as the vocal melody, hook, and words. Observe how the song breathes and breaks. Study it as if you were cramming for an exam.

As with any great music producer, you also need to develop a unique sound or niche. Something that makes your music stand out from the next producer but also not too far out so the average music goer won't be confused. You definitely don't want your tracks sounding like a pre-programmed demo for a sound module so this is where the creative work begins. It's not hard to tell an East coast Hip-Hop song from West coast. It's also not hard to tell a Kanye West, Timbaland, or Pharrell track from a Dr. Dre production. When it comes to Hip-Hop, even labels have their own unique identities such as Bad Boy Records, Death Row Records, Etc.   To become a great music producer, you must think and be on the level of these examples.

Another component is vision. Find the theme and point of your song and commit to it fully by using the right sounds, elements, lyrics, and melody to help paint your landscape. If you notice, great record producers aren't also afraid to take risks by being innovative, creative, and daring with their music. Every producer develops a sound and style or niche in the music industry, some styles are more prominent and mass appealing than others but originality is definitely a key, deciding factor to longevity and recognition. Don't be afraid to try something new, or make mistakes. Remember, there are no mistakes when creating.

One of the most deciding factors to getting hired by a record company as a producer could be based solely on your unique sound.

You may not necessarily have a long successful track record but the record company may believe your sound or style of music will sell to consumers. Another factor could be, a unique producer's sound may gel perfectly with one of their artists, when collaborated, could lead into major success for all three, the artist, producer, and record company. Signing on as an in-house producer or part of a production team could also be another factor in being hired as a producer. Your affiliation with the label or production company will allow you to co-produce with more seasoned and veteran producers until you're able to branch out on your own.

Chapter 11

Breach and Contract Violations

Overview

- Breach of producer agreements
- What is cease and desist
- Copyright infringement
- Examples of legal documents

Contracts and agreements are only in place just in case one party does not fulfill his or her obligation; this is called a "breach of contract". There are repercussions and penalties for not performing in compliance to your signed agreement. Sometimes you can be in violation by breaking the law unknowingly. Some violations could be copyright infringement, trademark infringement, piracy, and unauthorized duplication and replication. There are thousands of laws in the world of entertainment and especially in the field of production.

Once an artist is signed to a label, the label usually owns the artist's name, likeness, voice, and master recordings. If you infringe upon any of these cases, the label will send the culprit what's called a "cease and desist" known as "infringement letter" or "demand letter."
This is a document sent to an individual or business to halt purportedly unlawful activity ("cease") and not take it up again later ("desist"). The letter may warn that if the recipient by deadlines set in the letter does not cease and desist specified conduct, or take certain actions, that party may be sued.

I once released a song with a signed artist without permission and within 24 hours I received this cease and desist from Atlantic Records. In addition to Atlantic Records sending it to my

Attorney, and myself they also sent it to radio stations, Digital marketing companies, and anyone that supported this song in any format. They even contacted my digital distributor, which was Tunecore at the time and I was also fined a small amount. I could have been persistent and continued to promote and exploit this unauthorized song which would have been a very bad decision on my part, the next step would have been an injunction filed with the courts "a judicial process or order requiring the person or persons to whom it is directed to do a particular act or to refrain from doing a particular act, which would then lead to a lawsuit and more penalties for damages. No one wants to be in the media and blogs labeled as a thief or for being sued over a copyright that isn't yours.

There have been many copyright infringement cases throughout the history of music, sometimes the artist will actually take the writer's music or words and not acknowledge them with credit or a writers share so the writer's proceed to sue them. Most of the times, the original writers Are victorious with these cases and settle for way more than the profit, which was made. They are usually given a nice chunk in punitive damages to go along with the copyright infringement. One artist, which you may be familiar with is the Lauren Hill's lawsuit where Ms. Hill lost the case and was ordered to pay millions out to the original writers.

How do you avoid infringement cases? Write your own song material and fill out your split sheets immediately as the song is complete which will help eliminate and future disputes. Fill out your copyright form and register with Washington D.C. as soon as possible then you will be protected. There are countless writers and producers whom did not fill out their paperwork and lost their infringement cases so protect yourself. Like I said, credit is all you have so make sure you earn everything in which you're entitled to.

Cease and Desist Example 1

The first "Cease and Desist" example is an actual document in which I initiated the claim over a song produced and co-written by myself. My claim was against the artist for releasing my material on Soundcloud and the Internet without my permission. A lot of new musicians are unaware that the Internet and all platforms are included within the realms of unauthorized release and exploitation. If you feel that your rights are infringed upon, hire an attorney to draft a cease and desist, this shouldn't cost more than a few hundred dollars for your protection.

Cease and Desist Example 2

The second "Cease and Desist" Below is one in which Atlantic Records sent me involving one of their artist's. It was resolved within 48 hours and everything was fine afterwards. The digital distributor removed the content and fined me. As novice or beginner to experienced or expert. Everyone, besides a few genius exceptions, starts as a novice and learn to perfect and hone their craft through hobby experience, interning, formal training, or reading. You may study 10 years to learn the ropes of a music producer but still may not be or become successful as a producer. But why?

Cease and Desist Example 1

15th Floor
New York, New York 10019

ADAM L. KAPLAN
Attorney at Law

August 19, 2003

VIA EMAIL

Re: Tony Dofat as Producer and Writer of the composition ▓▓▓▓ / as performed by ▓▓▓▓ / Notice of Unlawful Reproduction and Exploitation.

Dear Mr. ▓▓▓▓:

The purpose of this letter is to inform yourself, ▓▓▓▓ (the "Infringing Parties") that my client, Mr. Tony Dofat, never provided Jack Straw Creative Agency, LLC, or any of the Infringing Parties, authority to mechanically reproduce and/or commercially exploit the composition ▓▓▓▓ (the "Composition") which was co-authored and produced by Mr. Tony Dofat.

We have been informed that ▓▓▓▓ LLC has unlawfully exploited said Composition on to Soundcloud and presumably other websites of interest. Since the exploitation of Composition by the Infringing Parties to date has been done so unlawfully, I hereby demand on behalf of my client that the Infringing Parties immediately cease and desist from any further exploitation of said Composition. Please be advised that any further exploitation whether via live performance, internet, or otherwise, by the Infringing Parties of the Composition produced by Mr. Dofat, or any of the other compositions Mr. Dofat co-wrote and produced with Ms. ▓▓▓▓ ("Other Compositions") which are controlled, in whole or in part, by Mr. Dofat's publishing designee shall constitute a willful infringement of my client's rights under copyright, trademark and other applicable federal and state laws, and we shall seek to hold the Infringing Parties liable for all applicable damages arising from such willful infringement.

In addition, on behalf of my client, I hereby demand that by the end of business Friday, November 7, 2014:
1) ▓▓▓▓ LLC, may have entered into or substantially negotiated with respect to the Composition and/or Other Compositions, which were all written, in whole or in part, by Tony Dofat, and/or produced by Tony Dofat, and 2) ▓▓▓▓ LLC, provide this office with evidence as to any and all monies received by ▓▓▓▓ LLC, with respect to compositions written, in whole or in part, by Tony Dofat, and/or produced, in whole or in part, by Tony Dofat.

This letter is not intended to be a complete recitation of all facts and circumstances relevant to this matter, and nothing contained or omitted from this letter shall constitute a waiver or election of any of my client's rights or remedies at law or in equity, all of which are expressly reserved.

Very truly yours,

Adam L. Kaplan

ALK/ps

cc: Tony Dofat

Cease and Desist Example 2

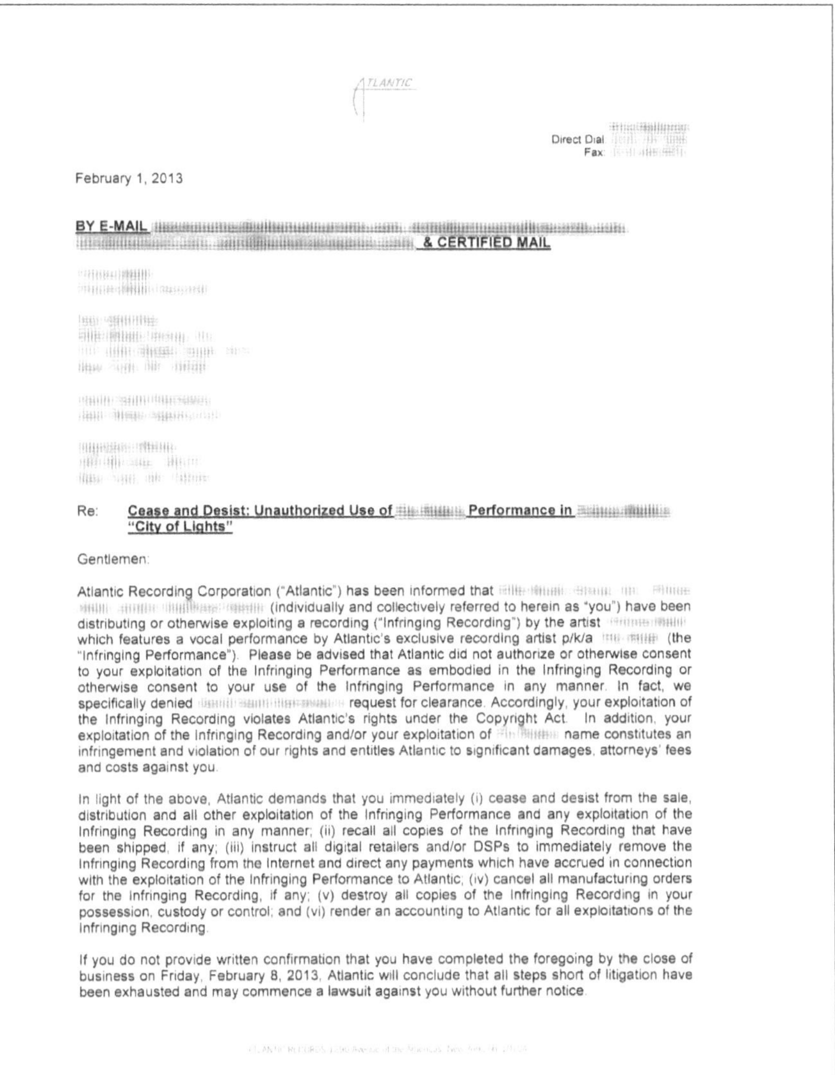

February 1, 2013

BY E-MAIL ▓▓▓▓▓▓▓▓▓▓▓▓▓▓▓▓▓▓▓▓▓▓▓▓▓▓▓▓ **& CERTIFIED MAIL**

Re: **Cease and Desist: Unauthorized Use of** ▓▓▓▓▓ **Performance in** ▓▓▓▓▓▓
"**City of Lights**"

Gentlemen:

Atlantic Recording Corporation ("Atlantic") has been informed that ▓▓▓▓▓▓▓▓▓ ▓▓▓▓▓▓▓▓▓▓▓▓▓▓ (individually and collectively referred to herein as "you") have been distributing or otherwise exploiting a recording ("Infringing Recording") by the artist ▓▓▓▓▓▓ which features a vocal performance by Atlantic's exclusive recording artist p/k/a ▓▓▓▓▓▓ (the "Infringing Performance"). Please be advised that Atlantic did not authorize or otherwise consent to your exploitation of the Infringing Performance as embodied in the Infringing Recording or otherwise consent to your use of the Infringing Performance in any manner. In fact, we specifically denied ▓▓▓▓▓▓▓▓▓▓▓ request for clearance. Accordingly, your exploitation of the Infringing Recording violates Atlantic's rights under the Copyright Act. In addition, your exploitation of the Infringing Recording and/or your exploitation of ▓▓▓▓▓ name constitutes an infringement and violation of our rights and entitles Atlantic to significant damages, attorneys' fees and costs against you.

In light of the above, Atlantic demands that you immediately (i) cease and desist from the sale, distribution and all other exploitation of the Infringing Performance and any exploitation of the Infringing Recording in any manner; (ii) recall all copies of the Infringing Recording that have been shipped, if any; (iii) instruct all digital retailers and/or DSPs to immediately remove the Infringing Recording from the Internet and direct any payments which have accrued in connection with the exploitation of the Infringing Performance to Atlantic; (iv) cancel all manufacturing orders for the Infringing Recording, if any; (v) destroy all copies of the Infringing Recording in your possession, custody or control; and (vi) render an accounting to Atlantic for all exploitations of the Infringing Recording.

If you do not provide written confirmation that you have completed the foregoing by the close of business on Friday, February 8, 2013, Atlantic will conclude that all steps short of litigation have been exhausted and may commence a lawsuit against you without further notice.

Cease and Desist
[redacted]
February 1, 2013
Page 2 of 2

Nothing contained herein shall expressly or impliedly constitute a waiver of any of Atlantic's rights, claims or remedies with respect to the subject matter hereof, all of which are hereby expressly reserved.

Sincerely,

[signature]

[name redacted]
Vice President, Business & Legal Affairs

cc: [redacted]

Chapter 12

The Record Label

Overview

- Operation and function of a label
- Major vs. Independent label
- Positions at a record label

What is a record label? Well, let's look at a record label as both a factory and bank combined. Their sole objective is to provide a loan to the recording artist for the manufacturing of a musical product; the technical term is known as a "Master recording". The artist advance, recording funds, promotional funds, marketing funds, and any other money paid out on the artist's behalf is considered a loan which you will have to pay back in full with an average profit split of 80-20, of course the label takes the 80%. One of the major difference between a record label and a bank is, when you go to the bank for a loan to buy a car or house, you will own that car or house after you pay off the loan. Unlike a record label, once you satisfy or "recoup" your loan with the Record Label, you will not own the item in which the loan was used for or the "master recordings". Artist's have figured this out and even more so once the digital era become the standard because you can actually record your own master recordings without loans for just a few hundred dollars. New artists have realized that it doesn't take too much to roll-out their own projects which would result in retaining Master ownership by bypassing the record label, We call this type of release or business model "independent" or Indie for short.

Why do you want to own your master recordings? Master recordings can become very valuable and can generate multiple revenue streams by way of sales, sync licensing, compilation albums, and sampling usage. Think of a Master Recording like a hotel, you may own the hotel but will rent a room to customers for any given time. After they're done with their stay, you can rent the same exact room to another customer. You will continue to own the hotel and will rent the same room as many times and as long as you want. A Master Recording operates by the same principles, you can rent or license the master usage as many times as you like and still continue to retain ownership. Let's say for example, your master recording tops the chart and becomes a hit, At this point, they can be worth millions of dollars.

What is the producer's role in this whole scheme? This industry is producer driven, producers are the ones to create and deliver the masters to the labels in which are created by a collaborative effort in conjunction with the recording artist. Record producers are like the middle- men between the label and the artist unless the artist is a producer. Major Labels will try to own everything including the producers thus the reason for offering them production deals or imprint deals which are basically a deal where the label will exclusively lock the producer in for a certain number of years and the producer must fulfill a commitment of a certain amount of master Recordings in which the label will own. The major Labels will entice the producers by calling it a label deal but it's not really a label because you, the producer, are not financing to manufacture the product and once your deal is complete you will not own the master recordings, However, you will get your logo printed on the product right next to the major label's logo and your label name would be included in conjunction with the major label. Producers have also figured out how to bypass the major labels and not get caught up by the up-front dollar signs dangling in front of their faces. In a perfect world, the artist and producer should and could collaborate without the involvement of a major label and both the artist and producer would co-own the master recordings and do a 50/50 net-profit share deal.

One of the first things that I've encountered as a professional producer was that the label and artists were always in disagreement with something. It took a while for me to understand that the larger labels are mostly about business and making money by any means necessary, even at the artist's expense. Actually, the labels are possibly 80 percent business and 20 percent creative but for the smaller boutique labels, the percentages are somewhat reversed. Smaller labels are controlled by creative executives and when I say "Creative" Executive, I mean the person or people in charge are actually creative, whether a producer or songwriter. They can actually pinpoint elements to enhance your music or direction and have studio or production experience.

Let's take a look at a few of the urban boutique labels, which sold millions of records and let's see who was in charge. Bad boy Entertainment was helmed by Entertainer and mogul/Producer Sean "Puff Daddy" Combs who's roster consisted of The Notorious BIG, Craig Mack, Faith Evans, 112, Total, Carl Thomas, Black Rob, The Lox, Mase, and the list goes on. Another boutique label was Irv Gotti's Murder Inc. with multi-platinum artists Ja Rule and Ashanti. So So Def was owned by Multi-Platinum Producer and artist Jermaine Dupree, Aftermath was owned by the West coast genius Dr Dre, Rapper Birdman owned and managed Cash Money Records, and Rapper Master P's imprint was "No Limit Records". These are just a few big names but these independent boutique labels were eventually acquired by the distributor or major labels. Now let's count on one hand, how many artists have been founded, developed, produced, and released by major labels alone. Not many and here's the reason why.

Major labels operate in a total different manner. The bulk of the labels consist of Marketing, promotion, business affairs, administration, accounting, and maybe 1 or 2 creative employees in which are not so creative but may have a few resources. Some employees are not familiar with marketing certain artist's, which leads to their project being shelved because of inexperience. How can someone that grew up in an upper class neighborhood market a rap artist from poverty stricken neighborhoods? They do not understand the art from these cultures, which is one of the reasons for the lack and downfall of creativity in today's hip-hop. Today's executives are to blame for not taking chances on great music, which is different from the current format but would rather sign an artist who sounds similar to another artist. The only way this will change is if we get more creative employees on staff and develop artists as we did in the 80's and 90's.

The protocol and positions at the major labels start from the scout or A&R, which is short for Artists and Repertoire. They act as the liaison between the label and the upper executives throughout the other departments. The A&R reports to the senior or Vice President of A&R, which is usually the Executive Producer. The Executive producer is the one over the entire creative process of the project. The EP (Executive Producer) or A&R are the key people to scout material for their projects and are the ones with the producer relationships. They may call on you to produce their next superstar but at the end of the day, it may never get released. Not because the song is not good but because the project may be placed on hold for years or indefinitely. Yes, as the producer you will still receive your advance but no one will be able to hear your work, which I like to refer to as art. There are numerous reasons why they may not want to rollout the project. The marketing department may not feel the talent is marketable enough. The promotions department may not receive the traction that was anticipated, or the artist may start to get frustrated and the label vs. Artist begins. The label will just chalk it off as a loss and move on to the next artist. One major executive referred artist's to cattle, he said, "Ship em in, ship em out."

Producers are not really affected by any artists vs. Label disagreements because we are considered a work for hire unless we have a song production commitment with the label but otherwise, we can reuse the material for another artist as long as your attorney add a reversion paragraph in your deal memo.

Chapter 13

The 360 Deal

Overview

* What is a 360 deal
* Pros and cons
* History of the 360 deal

The 360 deal has been around for quite some time, actually since the late 60's with Motown. It was not called a 360 deal but it was Motown's standard recording contract, to own the artist's touring and publishing rights. This concept was unfair and didn't work out well for the artist's advantage and eventually vanished until around 2002 with labels such as EMI and Atlantic Records. This was also during the beginning of the digital download era, which impacted sales, and loss of revenue for record labels.

The model for a standard record deal used to be; the label pays for production, marketing, promotion, and artist advance and in return the labels would solely own the masters and pay a small royalty (somewhere between 12-18 percent) however, with 360 deals, the labels recoup and profit from most of the artist's revenue streams include merchandise, tours and live performances, branding and/or endorsement deals and could include as much as publishing and films. The artist is usually paid a hefty advance, mostly in the millions, for relinquishing a portion of these rights. The digital era has attacked the labels and put them in a major crisis due to streaming services, Piracy, and digital downloads. Physical CD's are almost obsolete and music is being used to sell merchandise more than leisure enjoyment.

Let's take one of your favorite rappers for example. The label may spend $250,000 to record the album and an additional $500,000 to

Market and promote it. The artist may release and only sell 150,000 units, which will put the label deep in the red, meanwhile, the artist is getting paid from live performances, features, and appearances an estimated $350,000 per month from those revenue streams. Not only are they generating more revenue than the label but also they are using the label's budget to increase their popularity and to produce their product. Yes, the label will own their masters but master ownership is either a hit or miss. They may be worth something down the road or they may end up being worthless.

Some of the first groups to enter into successful 360 deals are the rock band Paramore, Madonna, and Jay-Z. Their deals were worth tens of millions. 360 deals have somewhat become the standard in today's major label signings and are not so terrible as people make them out to be, just make sure your attorney knows your potential worth and is familiar with 360 deal structures.

How does a 360 deal affect the producer? Your attorney should negotiate clauses in your deal memo or producer agreement regarding recoupment and specify what is deemed recoupable on your behalf, in order for you, the producer, to start collecting your royalties. In addition to the 360 deal, Brands are actually on the rise, creating music departments and developing and signing their own talent to promote their brand as well as compose original material for their products. Brands and corporations have found this model to be more cost effective and logical. Synchronization fees for song rights are expensive and artist's endorsement deals are even more expensive. I predicted this change maybe 10 years ago and it is finally coming to fruition in 2016. Record sales may have decreased but music is still valuable. Artist's popularity is very useful and these new model deals are based upon their audience level. Popularity is equated to audience, and audience level is equated to data collection and product sales. Data collection is just as important as making a sale. Obtaining detailed information about your audience can be sold and probably one of your most lucrative revenue streams. Social networks ask for so much personal information upon signing up and this data is used to market

Products to a specific demographic. For example; by liking a certain band or music, Facebook will promote a band similar to what you've liked in the past and not just limiting to music but everything. If you add, "Pet lover" to your interests, you will notice nothing but pet ads will appear on your newsfeed. Data collection is what makes Facebook so valuable and transformed into a Billion dollar corporation overnight.

Chapter 14

The Independent Record Label

Overview

- How to start a record label
- Tools needed to operate an independent label
- Why start an independent label

As the years go by, record labels are becoming more and more inessential. Artists and producers are purchasing portable DAW's and manufacturing their own music in less sophisticated manners. Realizing that label's revenue share is four times that of the artist by providing funding and a staff. Up until the late 90's, every artist's dream was to sign to a major but now in 2016, the tables have turned. Artists have realized that they do not need the labels and have proven that the labels need the artists. Most indie artist's can promote and market himself or herself better than most Harvard graduates with marketing degrees and at a fraction of the cost. I have been involved in plenty of indie start-ups so let's discuss the key factors.

Commercially satisfactory material – There is no need for million dollar recording facilities, home studios can be set-up in your bedroom (which I have done) and mixed at a properly tuned studio, this will save half of your budget without rushing and in the comfort of your own home.

Digital Distribution – By going exclusively digital, this step will totally wipe out the middleman, known as the record label. Going the digital route, you can easily get worldwide distribution via iTunes, Amazon, Spotify, Soundcloud, Etc. There will be no overhead charges for digital releases unlike physical distribution. If you decide to do a physical release, labels will charge back for CD color print & layout, thermal printing, and even shrink wrap (20 cents per CD), shipping costs, and one-sheets need to be created for the sales team.

Video Distribution – There are many platforms to host and promote your video for free or a very minimal cost such as VEVO, YouTube, and Zuus. You can shoot a great quality video on most DSLR's and also edit it for little to nothing. YouTube is a brilliant way to get discovered as with Justin Bieber and Greyson Chance and also costs $0.

New Media Marketing – Social networks, friends, followers, Vines, Twitter, Etc. are all very useful vehicles for free. If your material is good enough, you will build the traction and buzz to get noticed. People have become "Twitter" famous and some have received record deals because of their popularity. The rapper "Meek Mill" reached out to fellow rapper and Maybach Music's CEO Rick Ross to secured his record deal.

Online Publicity – This may be the only thing that could cost depending on the caliber of publicist. Sometimes you may be able to strike a deal for blog placement, press releases, and blurbs to promote your video and music. Blogs and website have millions of viewers daily and this exposure is very valuable. Let's take the popular website "Worldstar Hip-Hop ranks 247 in the United States by Alexa. Their daily traffic is over 1.2 million unique visitors per day so just imagine the exposure you will gain.

Websites – Websites are now inexpensive and there should be no reason why you shouldn't have one. Your website should be easily accessible and act as your main hub for fans. QR codes are a common thing nowadays and can be placed on just about any promotional item.

Club Rotation – There's nothing wrong with taking your song on a flash drive to a club and ask the DJ to play it at least one time. You may need some connections or resources to make this happen but this is effective as well.

Networking – Stay in the loop of things and go out with the sole purpose to mingle and network. You may meet people in which you can barter services or you may even collaborate with some other new artist's.

These steps are a great starting point and a cost effective way to monitor your traction. Remember that you are making music to hopefully build a fan base, which would eventually create a snowball effect in which you'd be able to monetize from. Most new artists follow these steps as their strategic plan to being noticed by a much larger, well-known artist or executive that can boost your music career. One of the most important pieces to the indie puzzle is having a great, dedicated team. Realize that everyone in this industry needs a team and although you may only see the artist shine, believe me, there is a team behind them.

Chapter 15

The Digital Era

Overview

* Digital vs. Analog
* Pros and cons
* How to manage with the digital era

As we turned into the new millennium, Analog along with the standard ways of doing things have slowly vanished and has been welcomed by the new era of the digital world. Things are now faster, more compact, easily accessible and better organized, and way more convenient being a fan of the digital era. Recording studios have now been converted into a laptop, headphones, and a USB controller with the luxury of non-linear and non-destructive recording at your fingertips. Let's be honest, is this actually better? My feelings on this subject are mixed and is a great topic up for a debate.

When people discuss the digital era, we tend to talk about just the pros of this transformation but what do we lose? Now that we have super high-speed internet and social networks, the average person does not have to actually communicate or interact personally with others which I feel is harmful to the millennia's social and communication skills. New-age audio engineers will never get the chance to feel what a knob on a piece of outboard gear or actual console faders feels like and in my opinion, this has harmed the quality of our art. Sonically, I do agree that our favorite songs do sound much better without tape hiss or record crackling but in return, we lose the feel that was present when the songs were created. There once was a time when we individually sampled and created drum sounds and also making our own personalized drum kits. This process was fun, tedious, and it made our sound unique as a producer. Today, drum kits are pre EQ'd and processed which are purchased by tens of thousands of aspiring producers resulting in a similar sound, worldwide, which lessens the quality and rarity of true art. When microwavable popcorn was first introduced, everyone went crazy, I compare today's music to just that, microwavable art. Our children of this generation is lacking the patience and diligence to micro manage and perfect their craft but should understand, things must ripen and mature over time before harvesting, but it's not their fault, they were just born into this era and this is all they know.

The digital era is also the blame for the decline of record sales, which results in the decline of mechanical royalties and digital streaming services has totally destroyed performance royalties. The music industry is a great career to do what you love but how is it possible to provide for a family with this mega decline in revenue? There are still other options and music will always be in demand, but for starters, you must expand your revenue streams to survive as a freelancer. Just think about how many commercials, sitcoms, reality shows Etc. you see on television and think about how many of them contain music. Probably 99.5 percent have scores and music beds, Which you can contribute to as a music producer and songwriter. The royalties from these sources are called synchronization rights or royalties and offer the most pay.

Just as I am defaming the digital world, I am also embracing it. I do have social media accounts, Facebook, Twitter, and Instagram. I use DAW's, plug-ins, control surfaces, Etc. I love the convenience of being able to digitally transfer full music sessions via the Internet in a matter of minutes across the globe, impressive. I use a lot of new digital platforms to promote and market my music or artist's for free as well, ingenious. I love the concept of non-destructive recording; this makes the job of and audio engineer 100 times easier and faster. As with everything else in life, balance is key. You must be versatile and balance the old with the new and you'll become unstoppable.

Chapter 16

Recording

Overview
- Get familiar with your DAW
- Studio equipment
- How to become a great engineer
- What is signal flow and audio chain

The recording process has been converted totally to digital, non-destructive and non-linear editing. Digital Audio Workstations, or DAW has been the industry standard since the late 90's; after Ricky Martin used pro Tools solely to record his #1 hit song "Livin La Vida Loca". This achievement made a tremendous impact on the recording industry. Understanding how DAW's work will give your recordings limitless possibilities. Some popular DAW's are Cubase, Logic, Abelton, and the most popular which is also the industry standard is Pro Tools. Why is non-destructive editing and recording ideal? You will never lose any of your recorded takes unless you intentionally delete them. You're also very much limitless with the amount of takes and tracks, which can be recorded or used simultaneously. There are many versions of Pro Tools; the software requires hardware in order to function. The hardware is known as your A/D converter or interface, which stands for "analog to digital" converter.

Why does someone need a converter? Well unlike analog technology which records audio waveforms as they are, these waveforms need to be converted to a digital format which is achieved by sampling analog waveforms thus converting them to a digital format. There are levels to the quality of your A/D conversion, for example; if you have the HDX A/D interface, your system will support a sample rate up to

192kHz (192,000 samples per second) and bit depth up to 64-bit, the highest quality of digital audio. These files sizes are very big and the quality is not much noticeable after your sample rate surpasses 44.1kHz (CD Quality) but higher sample rates are very precise for editing purposes. Another great feature with Pro tools is real-time effects processing. This allows your (plug-ins) effects parameters to be changed, altered, and edited in real-time without permanently affecting the original file. However, some DAW's do not require an A/D interface, which would limit some features such as; lower quality audio and less processing power.

Below is an example of a standard signal flow for digital Recording

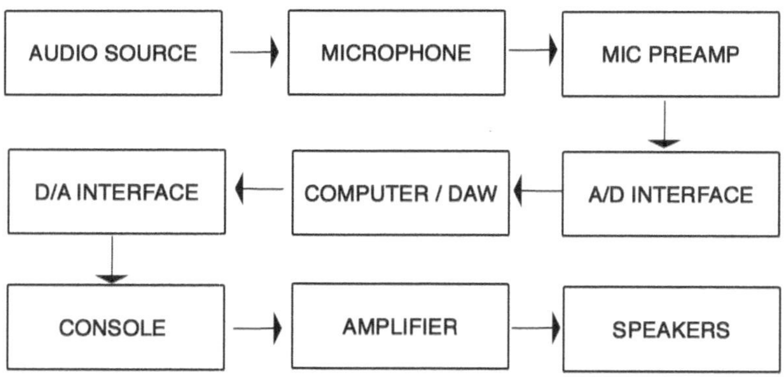

Signal flow is the path in which audio signal flows from the source to the output and there are multiple setups, depending on what you are recording. For example; recording a live guitar would have a different signal flow than a drum machine but once the signal enters the converter, the path from the converter to the output remains the same unless you are doing a live performance setup.

Becoming a great audio engineer comes with experience and a bunch of trial and error. Most great engineers follow the rules in which you were taught in audio school but almost every engineer breaks the rules after becoming comfortable in the professional world. Being great is not about following the rules but greatness is judged by your final result. Some traits of a great engineer are; you'd also have to work well with producers, artists, and understand the creative process. Your job is to sonically help with the vision of the producer. You must be organized by labeling, naming, and color-coding tracks along with song markers and notes. This will make things easier for the mix engineer, which will handle the session after you're complete with the recording. As an engineer, you usually start out as an intern after graduating and work your way up in-house until you have enough work credit and knowledge under your belt to become freelance.

One of the most important elements to recording vocals or instruments is your audio chain. An audio chain is the equipment in which your audio signal flows though prior to reaching your DAW. An audio chain would consist of standard studio outboard gear such as a microphone pre amp, compressor/limiter, equalizer, and a microphone.

Most engineers have their preference of equipment, the following is a list of some standard pieces of studio gear, which have been used for decades and is the preference for most top engineers throughout the world.

Microphones

- Sony C-800G
- Neumann U87
- AKG 414
- Neumann TLM103
- Neumann TLM170
- Neumann TLM193

Preamps & compressors

- Avalon VT737
- Universal audio 1176
- Universal audio 6176
- Neve 33609
- Neve 1073
- Neve 1081

Chapter 17

Mixing

Overview

- Get familiar with your DAW
- Studio equipment
- How to become a great engineer
- What is signal flow and audio chain

Now that we have a completed rough song, which is approved by the producer, Executive Producer, and artist, we have to do a final mix down of each individual track to create a stereo composite for mastering. Any Engineer is capable of doing a mix down but not advisable, the mix can turn a mediocre song into a hit if your mix engineer is good but it can also turn a hit song into a mediocre tune if your mix engineer is a novice or beginner.

Mixing comprises of equalizing the frequency of each sound to build a nice wide stereo image and simultaneously filling the entire frequency spectrum, ranging from 60 Hz or lower to somewhere around 14 kHz. If done correctly, the final result will give the song a more fuller and dynamic sounding mix, which is more appealing to the listeners and consumers. During the mix, the specially trained engineers will also add dynamics to each track by turning on plug-ins within the DAW, or by patching in outboard equipment if mixing analog. Dynamics will include EQ, compression, noise gate, De Esser, Etc. In addition to dynamics, the Engineer will also add effects such as reverbs, flangers, delays, stereo imaging, Etc. These effects will be used strategically to enhance the sound of certain instruments or vocal tracks. One of the luxuries with mixing in your DAW is real-time effect processing. This will allow you to alter the parameters

Of the effect thus changing the sound, in real-time without harming the source track.

The mix engineer will usually begin the mix by blending the drums first, then adding each instrument one at a time until all of the music tracks have been added. Once the producer and engineer are satisfied with the progression of the music, the vocals tracks will be added next. The background vocals must be blended properly to give a uniform feel and the harmonies must be placed at the exact level. Vocal mixing may take hours to complete due to the importance of the vocals, which is the most prominent component of a song. As tracks are added and blended, effects and dynamics are being adjusted and tweaked simultaneously until each track begins to mesh with the next. The mix engineer will monitor the sounds through various sets of speakers. Each set of speakers will output different frequency responses, meaning you may not be able to hear some sounds because the frequency of the sound may be too low or too high for that particular pair of speakers.

Mixes are very tedious and may take a full day or two to complete but when done correctly, even a beginner will be able to hear the difference. A great mix should vary from a wide stereo image to narrow and continue to move in and out throughout the song as background vocals play in and out. If you're a well-established mixer with an impressive track record, you may ask the label or artist for a royalty in conjunction to your fee, but under normal circumstances, mix engineers usually charge a flat fee per song.

Chapter 18

Mastering

Overview

- What is mastering
- What makes a great mastered song
- How important is the mastering stage

Mastering is the final stage for commercial music production prior to manufacturing, duplication, and distribution. Many people tend to misconstrue mixing with mastering but the two are totally different. Mastering is done in it's own facility called a Mastering house along with their own Engineers, specifically used for mastering. Mastering houses use special studio monitors, special equipment, and outboard gear specifically for mastering purposes. Various adjustments are made during this process, such as configuring the placement of the songs or sequence, the overall volumes are enhanced for consistent level with other released material in the market and for radio airplay and night club playback, the final touches are made to smooth mixes over and strengthen various elements in each track, volume fade-outs can be placed at the end and beginning of tracks, and other final adjustments are made to achieve the desired sound. This process creates the final versions of the recordings, typically known as the masters. After The Producer and Executive producer (s) approve the final product, the master would be sent to the duplication factory where physical CD's or vinyl is duplicated. Physical duplication has slowed down since the digital era but the mastering stage is still mandatory for digital downloads and radio/video play.

A great mastered song will sonically sound correct on various speakers such as your smartphone, laptop, car, or home stereo and

Throughout various locations, this is the goal of a mastering Engineer. Mastering a full album usually takes a full 8 hour day, depending on how many songs the engineer has to tweak and if last minute edits need to take place.

The mastering stage can actually make or break your song, which makes this a vital part of the record making process. An idea of a poorly mastered LP is; you're listening to an album at a specific and steady volume, one or more of the songs spike or dip in volume or a song is dull or brighter than the rest of the songs. Another example of a poorly mastered single can be easily heard in a nightclub. If your mastered song plays after an excellent mastered song, you will notice the drastic change in either volume or frequencies. Choosing a professional mastering house along with a top mastering engineer is crucial, do not trust someone with a DAW set-up in their bedroom portraying to be a mastering engineer because they may have purchased a mastering plug-in. There are plenty of decent mastering plug-ins but every song has unique frequencies, which should only be adjusted according to a trained human ear.

The following examples are two waveform images of an identical composition. One image shows the waveform of a mastered version and the other is a waveform of an un-mastered version. You can visually see the waveform difference; the mastered version appears to be louder and maximized as opposed to the un-mastered version.

These images below should reveal how important mastering is. The mastered version is more full and leveled properly which will give an end result of a commercially satisfactory product.

UNMASTERED

MASTERED

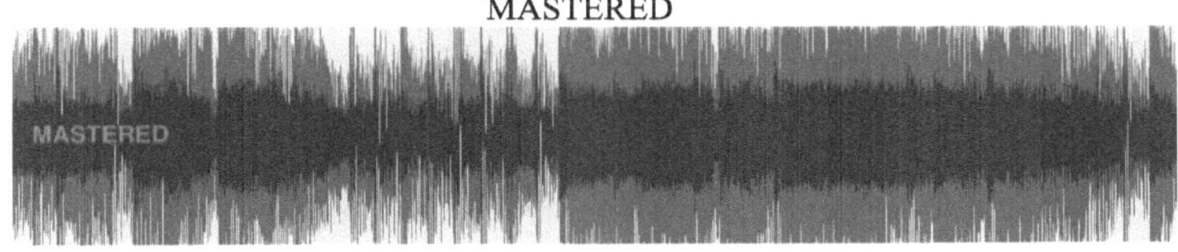

Chapter 19

Industry Quotes

- Treat everyone with respect because in this industry, an assistant can eventually become your boss.

- The industry is smaller than you think, make sure to handle business with proper ethics.

- Don't taint your reputation by owing or stealing money

- Let your team play their roles and don't over step boundaries

- Listen to your attorney

- If something's not broken then it doesn't need to be fixed

- Know that you don't know everything

- Hang around people in which you inspire to be

- Never make important decisions while under the influence or not in the proper state of mind

- Know who to trust with your unreleased music

- Balance your life, too much of anything is no good

- Get rid of those who bring negative vibes

- Hire a lawyer to oversee your lawyer

- Don't spend money before you receive it

- Don't live beyond your means

- Always be prepared to learn

- Remain humble, people don't like arrogance

- Never lose the value of a dollar

- Never take credit for someone else's work

- Always receive credit for your work, credit is all you have

- Know your worth

- Never discuss your finances publicly

- Believe in karma

- Love your enemies and haters; you lose all power when you react to their antics.

- Don't love what doesn't breathe

- Your life can change in a second by being at the right place and the right time

- The music business never sleeps

- Don't offer opinions in someone else's session without someone asking for it

- Mute your ringtone upon entering a studio session

- Do not have a full blown conversation in the studio with someone while your engineer is trying to mix

- It's ok to have a difference of opinion

- Being lazy and trying to cut corners will only make you do it twice

- Whatever you take for granted will eventually be taken from you

- Be careful what you wish for, it just might happen

- People are more likely to help you once you help yourself

- Always arrive early, real professionals respect time

- Never be afraid of failure

- Maintain great health, health is wealth

- Watch how people treat others; this will be an indication of how they will treat you.

- Travel as much as you can

- Swallow your pride and learn to accept criticism

- Know the difference between someone hating and sincere criticism

- Always remain an asset and never a liability

Biography

The year was 1992 and New York was on fire. From hip-hop to the big apple dominated the music scene, delivering raw, unparalleled talent from the boroughs to the mainstream. While infamous industry folk like Sean "P Diddy" Combs were in the forefront of developing legendary acts such as Mary J. Blige, a somewhat hidden genius lay in the cut quietly drumming out some of the craziest sounds heard round the world. Introduced to the music business through Diddy himself, this multifaceted Mt. Vernon, NY native went on to compose, arrange, mix, engineer and produce for over two decades.

Working on countless songs and remixes alongside the Bad Boy founder, Dofat created and produced hit tracks and remixes for everyone [to name a few] from Heavy D, Mary J. Blige, Queen Latifah, Will Smith, Black Rob, Method Man, and Jodeci to Tina Turner, Biggie and MTV's Da Band. Highly respected for his command of the recording studio and for his creative vision, Dofat is regularly called upon by the industry's leading icons including Andre Harrell, Diddy and Heavy D to consult on artist development and musical direction. Having produced, remixed, and released over 120 compositions with numerous Top Ten hits (42 RIAA certified Gold, Multi Platinum) he is without a doubt a powerhouse in his own right.

Working under the tutelage of Diddy at Bad Boy since its inception,

Dofat was a member of the crucial production unit, The Hit Men. In addition to creating a plethora of chart toppers for the Bad Boy roster, Dofat went on to tackle the big screen in 2001 with the release of a New York Times Critics choice Hip-Hop Documentary, "Street Dreams/Ballers". Produced & Directed by Dofat, under the banner of his Chinavision Films and distributed through a deal with Ventura/UrbanWorks Entertainment, the award-nominated documentary by Urban World Film Festival, Hollywood Film Festival, explored the world of rap music and the evolution of hip-hop culture as few had seen   before.

After years behind-the-scenes in the lab, this visionary connected his persona to his respected reputation when he appeared on MTV's Making the Band 2 and 4, where he was the primary entity assigned by Diddy to work directly with the hip-hop ensemble. Credited as Associate executive producer, record producer, musician, writer, and engineer/mix engineer, Dofat created Da Band's album, which debuted at #1 on the Billboard charts and was certified Gold in the first week of release, Dofat completed the project in less than eight weeks and produced the "Too hot for TV" studio album including the two lead singles "Badboy This, Badboy That" and "Tonight".

In 2009, Dofat's work was nominated for a Grammy Award with Heavy D's LP release, Vibes, contributing as Producer, co-Executive

Producer, Musician, and Mix Engineer.

Somewhere throughout the hectic production schedule and long studio hours, Dofat managed to tour the world and work on the live side of music as Musical Director and Pro Tools editor. Multi platinum Artists such as Diddy, Jay Z, Timbaland, Usher, Jagged Edge, Danity Kane, Day 26, Jamie Foxx, and many others called on Dofat regularly to arrange and mastermind their live performances.

Currently, Tony Dofat is an Associate Professor, Record Producer, Independent Consultation, and Audio & Mix Engineer.

My early beginnings – I made my official indulgence in music at the age of 9 as a trumpeter with my elementary school band. My undiscovered passion for music allowed me to instantaneously learn to read music and rapidly command the first trumpet, first chair position that I held throughout my 9 years of playing.

Developing my passion for music – As I grew older into my early teen years, I became intrigued with sounds contained in certain songs and the way it made me feel and react when I listened to it. With the likes of Kraftwerk, Talking heads, Duran Duran, Run DMC, LL Cool J, Marvin Gaye, James Brown, and Al Green just to name a few.

Business and Fundamentals of Music Production

Developing my passion to create – Not until my older teen years did I actually decide to inquire about creating music through the likes of producer Teddy Riley, Guy, Al B Sure, and Heavy-D.

My early creations – Starting without funding, I learned to make rough tracks and simple sequencing with entry-level music equipment. I recall some equipment to be an Alesis 8 track sequencer, Korg DDD-5 drum machine, Boss Dr Rhythm drum machine, and a Casio keyboard.

Perfecting my craft – During my late teens, after receiving critique from my peers and developing an even stronger passion for creating music, I realized that I had a small amount of potential and began to place music higher on my priority list. I would create tracks daily and started to realize, music had a place in my heart.

Networking – I began to network with entry-level writers and others with the same desire and passion to pursue the music industry. I had a neighborhood friend whom believed in my passion and talent and decided to partner with me. We purchased professional music equipment, and started developing local artists such as Case and DMX.

Developing a sound – Being influenced by the current Hip Hop of the 80's and also the soul greats from the 70's including

Commodores, Sly & the Family Stone, Ohio Players, Marvin Gaye, Al Green, James Brown, I began to develop a unique sound by combining hip hop and soul music. It felt so natural for me to create a Hip-Hop beat with an R&B feel.

Making My Connection – My early 20's, after spending countless hours, days, and months teaching myself, making music, and recording on my Tascam analog 8-track recorder I began to gain the likes of many locals and undeveloped artists. I was proposed by another one of my childhood friends to partner with Sean Combs aka Puffy or Puff Daddy. Sean was from my small hometown, Mount Vernon, N.Y. and had just landed an internship with the Andre Harrell's Uptown/MCA Records. He received a cassette of my music from a mutual friend and was impressed with my sound so he stopped by my studio and said, "Let's work! "Do you make some records?" he asked. Anyone aspiring to make music professionally would answer, "yes" as which I did. We had nothing to lose and everything to gain by taking a chance with a success ratio of about 1 in a million.

Entering The Music Business – The date was September 1992, we were 100% analog during these days, and our first session was about a few days after we initially met up. Puffy called me earlier that day to give me the studio address, which was 254 West 54th Street in NYC, The Hit Factory. This was my first professional session, which happened to be on a Neve VR72 flying fader console. My engineer was Tony Maserati, a recent graduate from Boston's Berklee College of Music. Little would I know that he'd be a multi Grammy award winner known for mixing some of the hugest artists in the industry, from R Kelly to Beyoncé. The artist was also in the studio, her name was Mary and she was just quietly sitting in the chair. My equipment of choice was the Akai MPC 60 II, Roland SBX 80 Sync box, Korg M-1 and a Roland D-70 keyboard. The outboard gear that we used was Lexicon PCM 42 delays, Eventide H-3000 Ultra harmonizer, Yamaha SPX 90, Pultec EQ, a few DBX 160's, and UA 1176. I sampled drum sounds into the MPC directly from vinyl then truncated and sequenced within the MPC 60. Our tape machine was a 2 inch analog Studer A827 24 track and running at 30 IPS. The song was recorded and mixed within the same night and approximately 16 hours later, we were done!

This was our first time in a professional studio and was totally clueless but did understand and knew what good music was. We had no idea that history was being made that night but as you can see from my detail, it was probably my most memorable session to date. Not knowing that history was being made, about a week later, I hear our song blasting from cars driving by as well as the radio. Everyone loved the song and this launched our careers from zero to a hundred overnight. Mary J Blige's "You Remind Me" will always bring back these memories.

Visual Memoir 1992-2016

Discography

ARTIST	LABEL	ALBUM	SONG(S)
8Ball & MJG ▲▲	Universal	Lost "Bonus"	McGruff "Many Know"
AZ	Virgin	Pieces of A Man	Betcha Don't Know
Baby ●	Cash Money	Birdman	Do That Dance (Mix)
Bell Biv Devoe	Universal	BBD	Breezy
Black Rob	Virgin Records	Wendy Williams "Bring The Heat"	Warrior
Black Rob	Badboy Records	The Black Rob Report	They Heard I Got Life Watch Your Movements w/Akon Fire In Da Hole w/Ness Team Warrior
Bozz Skaggs	Virgin	Single	I'll be the one (remix)
Brian McKnight	Mercury	Single	I Can't Go For That (remix)
Carl Thomas ▲	Badboy Records	Emotional	Hey now (mix)
Champ M.C.	East West Records	Ghetto Flava	Funk House Cruisin Catchin' Wreck Niggaz? Murder Mine Time 2 Roll Stressin' Me
Cheryll Pepsii Riley	Warner Bros.	All That!	I'll Be There
Christopher Williams	Uptown	Changes	Let's Get Right
Da Band ●	Bad Boy records	2 Hot 4 TV	We Here Living Legends My Life How U Like Me Now Tonight I like Your Style Why Badboy This Badboy That Stick Up Hold Me Down They Know
Da Band ●	Badboy Records	2 Hot 4 TV	Holla Whatcha Be Doin Go Steady
Da Band ▲	Badboy Records	"Bad Boys II" Soundtrack	Why
Damion Hall	Silas/MCA	Single	Satisfy You
E.V.E.	MCA	Single	Groove Of Love
El Debarge	Warner Bros.	Heart, Mind & Soul	Special Lady
Eric Gable	RCA	Process of Elimination	Don't Won't To Hurt Nobody
Father M.C.	Uptown	Single	One Night Stand f/Mary J. Blige (remix)
Heavy D	Universal	"In Progress"	*So Sexy *Creepin' *Touch Me

Heavy D	Uptown/ Universal	"Heavy"	Spanish Fly Don't Stop You Know *w/Cee-low* Dancin' In the Night Ask Heaven On Point *w/Pun & Eightball* Anything You Want I Know You Love Me Like Dat Dhere Imagine That
Heavy D ●	Uptown/Universal	Waterbed Hev	Big Daddy Big Daddy (remix) Keep It Comin' Keep it Comin' (remix) Shake It I'll Do Anything Don't Be Afraid *w/Big Bub* Wanna Be A Playa *w/McGruff* Come and Get It *w/Soul for Real* Can You Handle It *w/Dog Pound*
Heavy D	Untertainment	"Woo" Soundtrack	Take a Ride *f/McGruff*
Heavy D ●	Uptown/MCA	Blue Funk	Who's The Man Who's The Man (remix) Truthful Who's in The House
Heavy D ▲	Uptown/Universal	U.S. Single	Big Daddy
Heavy D	Stride/Universal	Vibes	Long Distance Girlfriend Chasing windmills
Heavy D	Stride/Universal	Love Opus	Still missing you
Jada Pinkett-Smith	Overbrook	My Story	My Story
JaRule	Fontana/UMG	PIL2	F*ck Fame
J-Shin	Southbeat	All I Got is Love	Caught Up
Jodeci	Uptown/MCA	Single	I'm Still Waiting- Something For The Jeeps (remix)
Keith Sweat	Elektra	Single	Love You Down (remix)
Lorenzo	Alpha Intl.	Single	Make Love To Me (remix)
Mad Cobra	EMI	Milkman	It's A Shame
Mary J. Blige ●	Uptown/MCA	Single	You Remind Me *f/Greg Nice* (remix)
Mary J. Blige ▲ ▲ ▲ ▲	Uptown/MCA	"What's the 411"	What's the 411 Leave A Message Intro Talk Sweet Thing (remix) Don't Wanna Do Anything Else (remix) Love No Limit (remix)
Mary J. Blige ▲	Uptown/MCA	"What's the 411" Remix Album	You Don't Have To Worry *f/Craig Mack* (remix) You Don't Have To Worry *f/Craig Mack* You Remind Me *f/Greg Nice*
McGruff	Uptown/Universal	Destined To Be	Before We Start Gruff Express Many Know How We Do…*f/Lost Boys* What Part of The Game *f/Panama PI, Cam'ron*

Business and Fundamentals of Music Production

Men of Vizion	MJJ/Sony	"Personal"	Housekeeper (remix)
Method man ●	Def jam Records	Tical 0 : The Prequel	Say What *f/ Missy Elliot*
Monifah ●	Universal	Mohogany	I'm Lovin' You Would You Be Touch It (remix)
Monifah	Qwest/Warner Bros.	"Sprung" Soundtrack	I Still Love You
Monifah	Uptown/Universal	Moods Moments	You (remix)
Montell Jordan ●	Def Jam	More…	Tricks on My Mind
Ness	Badboy Records	U.S. Single	My Hood
Notorious BIG ▲ ▲ ▲	Badboy/Arista	Born Again (Jpn)	Niggaz
Notorious BIG ▲ ▲	Badboy/Atlantic	Duets	B.I.G. LIVE in Jamaica (Intro)
Olivia *	Wonda Music	TBD	Animal Attraction
Papa Chuck	Pendulum records	Badlands	Down n dirty
Pudgee the fat bastard	Giant Records	Give em tha finger	Keep ur coat on
Queen Latifah ●	Motown	Black Reign	Listen 2 Me Rough Bring The Flavor Can't Understand
Rough House Survivors	Relativity	Rough House	Take A Trip Can U Dig It? So! Survivors We Can Rhyme Straight From The Soul On The Flex Rough House Check Da Back Pack Once Again
Screen Scene	B.E.T. Cable Network		Screen Scene Theme
Shinehead	Epic Records	Single	Jamaican in NY (remix)
Skin Deep	Loose Canon/ PolyGram	Get You Open	Joy Ride Supastar
Soul For Real	Uptown/Universal	For Life	Stay You Just Don't Know *f/Heavy D* Love You So (remix)
Sybil	Next Plateau	Single	We (remix)
The Next Afternoon	Showtime	Opening Score	Heist
Tina Turner	Virgin	"What's Love Gotta Do With It" Soundtrack	Why Must We Wait Until Tonight (remix)
Vanessa Williams	Mercury/PolyGram	Single	The Way That You Love Me (remix)
Will Smith ●	Sony Music	Born to Reign	Willow is a player
Winans	Qwest/Warner Bros.	"Extra Mile"	That Extra Mile (remix)

Glossary

360 Deals
Also referred to as "multiple rights deals", 360 deals are exclusive recording artist contracts that allow a record label to receive a percentage of the earnings from ALL of a band's activities instead of just album sales. Under this type of contract, a record label is entitled to a percentage of multiple revenue streams, most of which were previously off limits in a recording contract, such as live concert fees, merchandise sales, endorsement deals, book and movie deals, ringtones, private copying levy royalties, etc., as well as the music publishing rights and revenues of the Artist/Composer(s).

AAC
Advanced Audio Coding (AAC) is a digital file format similar to MP3. Its probable best-known use is as the default encoding system used by Apple's iTunes.

A&R
The A&R (Artist and Repertoire) department in a record company is responsible for spotting, nurturing and developing new artists as well as acting as a point of contact for existing ones. They work closely with the artists throughout recording projects, in conjunction with managers, producers, songwriters and other musicians.

Adaptation
A new version of a song that is inspired by an original work whether by different interpretation or instrumentation.

Administration
The practice and process of business functions relating to a catalogue of works or individual works, collection and distribution of fees and royalties, and all other responsibilities that relate to the use of a musical work and/or sound recording.

Advance

An advance is a loan, normally from a record label to an artist, to be repaid (recouped) from record sales. An advance is for one or more albums depending on the contract. A publisher's advance would be recouped from publishing royalties.

AFM

American Federation of Musicians, commonly referred to as the "Musician's Union".

Agent

Music agents, otherwise known as booking agents, are the people who help make the live music happen. A good agent with well-placed connections can help get a band in front of the right audience to increase their profile. Agents work closely with promoters and record labels to get the bands on their books the proper exposure. Music agents also negotiate with promoters and venues for performance contracts and arrangements for things like backline and accommodation.

Aggregator

A company that collects and organizes music; normally an online music distributor (i.e. CDBaby, Tunecore, IODA, The Orchard, etc.)

Arrangement

A modification of an existing composition. Arrangements can be copyrighted separately from the compositions they reference. When that happens, both the arranger and the composer receive royalties. One of the protections the copyright law gives musicians is the exclusive right to arrange their compositions, so it is illegal to arrange a copyrighted work for distribution without permission from the composer.

Arranger

A person who writes musical arrangements. Arrangements can be copyrighted separately from compositions. When that happens, both the arranger and the composer receive royalties.

ASCAP

American Society of Composers, Authors and Publishers is a performing rights organization (see definition below) in the US.

Assignment

Copyright can be assigned to a label or publisher, or a third party such as a royalty collection society for a period of time. This allows the assignee to act on behalf the copyright owner to issue licenses and collect royalties within the terms of the assignment

Audit

An audit is the process of reviewing and analyzing financial records from record labels and music publishers. Audits are undertaken on behalf of the contracted recording artist and/or composer. An audit clause is a term in an agreement or other legal document that authorizes one party to audit another.

Author

A creator of an artistic, literary, musical or dramatic work.

BDS (Broadcast Data Systems)

A service that tracks monitored radio, television and internet airplay of songs based on number of spins and detections. BDS captures in excess of 100 million song performances occurring on more than 2,000 radio, satellite radio, network radio, and music video channels across North America.

Black Box Income

In the music industry context, this term refers to royalty income, usually mechanical royalty income from foreign territories that has not yet been collected by the Publisher, or royalties that cannot be attributed to specific works or copyright owners. This income may come from the result of audits, adjustments or international sources.

Barcode

A barcode is a machine-readable number (e.g. UPC code) used for various purposes in manufacture, retail and commercial use of CDs and Vinyl. Barcodes don't just identify CDs at the counter, they are also used for chart returns. Some distributors and retailers insist on barcoding.

Blanket License

A license issued by a performing rights society that authorizes the public performance of all the songs in the society's catalog. This allows the licensee to perform as many or as few of the titles as desired.

BMI

Broadcast Music, Inc. is a performing rights organization in the US. BMI collects royalties for publishers and writers.

Business Manager

A person who helps a musician with financial planning, investment decisions, tax matters, monitoring of income and other financial matters.

Cassette Tapes

Cassette tapes were the standard media for delivery of music through retail channels during the 'seventies and 'eighties. Mechanical licenses may apply to your tape recordings.

Census

An analysis of ALL music used by a licensee during a specific reporting period.

Clearance (copyright)

For the right to use music in some circumstances it must be cleared with the copyright owners. Clearance is needed for copying, not just for commercial use. It is normally negotiated through licensing and collection societies, but may be collected through labels and publishers.

Compact Discs

Compact discs have been the standard media for delivery of music through retail channels for at least a decade. Mechanical licenses may apply to your CD recordings.

Composer
A creator of music and melody. The individual who wrote the song, found at the top right of the title page and used to identify a copyrighted work. Often multiple songs share the same title. So this is necessary to locate the proper copyright holder of a song. It is also required information under the compulsory mechanical licensing provisions.

Controlled Composition
A clause in many North American recording contracts in which the recording artist, as a songwriter, agrees to a reduced mechanical royalty rate (usually 75% of the current rate), if the songs on an album are composed by the artist themselves.

Co-Publishing Agreement
A type of publishing agreement whereby two or more publishers will share in the ownership of a copyright for a specific work or body of works Typically, one publisher will have full administration rights. This type of publishing agreement often applies in cases where the composer is a recording artist or producer.

Copy Protection (CD)
Major record labels used to use a number of different (so-called) copy protection techniques for certain releases. These are formatted in a non-standard way to stop them playing normally in PCs.

Copyright
Exclusive rights to a work, including the sole right to publish, produce, reproduce, translate, communicate to the public by telecommunication and, in some cases, rent a work. It also includes the right to perform a work in public, and under certain conditions, to exhibit in public an artistic work.

Copyright Registration
A record stating the creation date of a work and its content, so that in

the event of infringement or plagiarism, the copyright owner can produce a copy of the work from an official source.

Cover Record
Another version of a song that already exists by a different artist

Covers (copyright)
Anyone can cover another writer's work, under the terms of PRS or MCPS assignments where they exist. Under these blanket licenses the writer is paid mechanical and performance income. If the work is not assigned to MCPS or PRS the cover should be cleared through the publisher. This rule applies unless the original work has not been covered before, and if this is the case permission must be granted by the original artist or their publisher.

Creative Commons
This term refers to both an organization and a set of licenses. The Creative Commons organization is a non-profit organization headquartered in the US devoted to expanding the range of creative works available for others to build upon legally and to share. Creative Commons license are those licenses issued by the Creative Commons, which depending on which version is used, removes some of the restrictions of normal copyright protection (i.e. some rights reserved). With a Creative Commons license, the creator and/or copyright owner may still keep their copyright but may also allow people to copy and distribute their work provided they give proper credit (attribution) and only on the conditions specified in the particular version of the license being used. Some Creative Commons licenses allow the public performance of a sound recording and musical work but only for non-commercial purposes. However, a copyright owner may already have pre-assigned these rights in which case these rights would be reserved and not granted under a creative commons license.

Cross Collateralization
A clause in recording and publishing agreements allowing the record-

ing or publishing company to recoup outstanding advance balances from one album release with revenues from the next forthcoming release(s) and/or in the case of a multiple rights deal (i.e., a 360 deal) from various sources such as music publishing royalties, concert fees, merchandise sales, etc.

Cue
Music used in the context of a television or film production.

Cue Sheet
A document that itemizes music used in a television or film production by title, composer, publisher, duration and type of music usage (e.g., background, feature, and theme). The cue sheet is normally prepared by the producer of the television or film production.

DAI – Digital Audio Identification
The use of pattern recognition, or "fingerprinting", to identify musical works aired on radio, by attempting to match them against a BDS library of known works.

Demo
A sample recording of a band's music. Often rough recordings or early versions of "songs in progress."

Derivative Work
Commonly a US copyright term, it is a new work derived from one or more pre-existing works, such as a remix of a song, acoustic version, or a song based on a poem, etc. For derivative works, the original copyright holders may have a claim in the new version even if they are not the creators of the derivative work. A copyright owner reserves the right to authorize a "derivative work" based upon one or more pre-existing works, such as a translation, musical arrangement, dramatization, fictionalization, motion picture version, sound recording, a remix, art reproduction, abridgment, condensation, or any other form in which a work may be recast, transformed, or adapted.

Digital Download

The process of transferring a digital file from one computer to another. For music, MP3 is the most popular format, although one may now have the option of buying high quality FLAC lossless files.

Digital Phonorecord Deliveries
Permanent digital downloads (also known as Digital Downloads or DPDs) and are treated like CD sales. DPDs reside on a recipient's computer indefinitely. DPDs may be transferred to portable devices or burned onto CDs (in accordance with the rules set by the digital distributor of a specific DPD). DPDs fall under U.S. Copyright Act and are currently licensed at the statutory rate. Mechanical licenses apply to DPDs.

Disintermediation
The elimination of intermediaries in the supply chain, which is also referred to as "cutting out the middleman". In the music business, mostly due to the opportunities and low cost associated with using the Internet to market, sell and distribute music to an artists' fans directly, this term refers to "creator to consumer" without the aid of, cost of, a traditional third-party "middleperson" i.e. a record label.

Distribution
The delivery of product from manufacturing to the user. Distribution happens whenever product leaves possession of the licensee, regardless of whether it is sold or given away for free. Often labels will approach a distributor to act as a middleman between themselves and retailers. Traditional distribution is about taking orders for and supplying CDs (or other physical product) from record labels to retail, although their role can be more complex and they may also promote and invest in releases. Digital distributors (see 'Aggregators') serve online stores (such as iTunes) in a similar fashion, handling downloadable releases by many labels at the same time and ensuring they are supplied to all the different online outlets.

DRM (Digital Rights Management)
DRM technologies attempt to control the use of digital media by preventing access, copying or conversion to other formats by consumers

and their peers. In terms of music, DRM technologies are used in cases where the copyright owner chooses to control the ways in which content (in a recording, for instance) is used or misused. This usually is an attempt to stop illegal copying, "ripping" or file sharing.

Endorsement
This is a promotional tactic employed by equipment manufacturers in which they provide gear at discounted prices (sometimes even free of charge) to high profile and successful artists in exchange for exposure generated by the artist's use of the product.

EP
Extended Play (EP) records were originally 3 or 4 track 45 rpm 7 inch vinyl singles. (A normal vinyl single had one track on each side.) These days the term EP is used to describe releases that have more than two tracks but are too short to qualify as a full studio album or LP which usually contains at least 10 tracks.

Exclusive Rights
The privileges that only a copyright owner has with respect to the copyrighted work.

Exploit
To seek sources and opportunities leading to gain of revenue for a song or artist.

Fair Use
A doctrine in US copyright law allowing limited use of copyrighted material without requiring permission from copyright owners for such uses as commentary, criticism, news reporting, research, teaching or scholarship. A similar principle, Fair Dealing (see definition above), exists in some other common law jurisdictions such as Canada.

FLAC – Free Lossless Audio Codec
A file format for audio data compression that does not remove information from the audio stream, as MP3, AAC and Vorbis.

Format
The medium for delivery of the music. Common formats include
Digital Downloads, CDs, Records, and Cassette Tapes.

Gracenote
A metadata base provider used with an application called CDDB
(short for "Compact Disc Data Base"). When you insert a CD into
your computer and iTunes starts, the iTunes application sees the CD,
and makes a request over the Internet to the CDDB application "asking" if it "knows" what CD has been inserted into the computer. If
the answer is yes, then CDDB returns information about the release
(Artist Name, Track Titles, etc....) back to iTunes, and iTunes then
displays this information in its main window.

Grand Right
The legal rights necessary to stage an opera, play with music, or a
work of musical theater.

Harry Fox Agency
The Harry Fox Agency (HFA) is an organization that represents music publishers for mechanical and digital licensing in the US. It issues
licenses and collects and distributes royalties on behalf of its affiliated
publishers. This includes licensing for the recording and reproduction
of CDs, ringtones and Internet downloads. HFA does not issue synchronization (or synch) licenses for the use of music in advertising,
movies, music videos and television programs after 2002. HFA also
conducts royalty examinations, investigates and negotiates new business opportunities, and pursues piracy claims.

Indie (Independent)
Normally refers to a band or performer not affiliated with or owned
by a major label.

Intellectual Property
A form of creative endeavor that can be protected through a copyright, trademark, patent, industrial design or integrated circuit
topography.

Interpolated Work
A song that is not written expressly for an audio-visual production but is taken from an outside source (e.g., recording) and used within that production.

ISRC
International Standard Recording Code. This is an international identification system for sound recordings and music videos. Each ISRC is a unique and permanent identifier for a specific recording that can be permanently encoded into a product as its digital "fingerprint". Encoded ISRCs provide the basic means to automatically identify recordings for royalty payments.

Jingle
A short musical piece normally used on radio to identify or to advertise content.

Length of Song
The length of your recording of a song in minutes and seconds is required information under the compulsory mechanical licensing provisions. Songs over five minutes cost a little higher royalty.

Library of Congress (part of Copyright Registration)
A federal cultural institution in the US. Located in Washington D.C., it receives copies of every book, print, and piece of music registered in the country.

License
A legal agreement granting someone permission to use a work for certain purposes or under certain conditions. A license does not change the ownership of the copyright.

License Fee
Fees that are charged for the licensed use of a copyright-protected work
Re: other uses - a fee (can be a negotiated one-time, buy-out or variations) for the specific use of a copyrighted work as outlined in the License agreement between the copyright owner (or representative) and the user.

LP
Long Play (LP) are 33⅓ rpm microgroove vinyl records and are a format for phonograph (gramophone) records, an analog sound storage medium. They are also known as albums as one vinyl record would replace several of the shorter-running 78 rpm records. LP's usually contains at least 10 songs or tracks.

Major Label
The original definition of a 'major' was a record company, which also owned manufacturing and distribution facilities. The ownership and structure of all the majors has changed since the definition was first coined but still the 'big four' (in terms of market share – Universal, Sony, EMI and Warner) are commonly identified by this term.

Manufacture
The making of copies of music. For example, when CDs are duplicated, they are in manufacturing.

Marketing
The process of aiming to increase artist popularity, profile and product sales by generating interest in the artist's music. This includes exposure in various mediums such as print, television, radio and the Internet.

Mash-up
A mash-up is a song or composition created by blending or mixing two or more songs together, normally resulting in the layering of the vocal track of one song seamlessly over the music track of another. In the end, a mash-up is a "new" work consisting entirely of the combi-

nation of other works. Commonly this is two different works layered over one another to draw comparison of similar styles and sounds in both works. Master (sound recording) The final mixed and mastered recording. The source from which copies are made.

Mastering

Mastering is the process of preparing the final mix of a song or album for duplication. The final process of preparing a mixed recording for commercial distribution. Various adjustments are made during this process, such as configuring the playing order placement of the songs, the overall volumes are enhanced for consistent level with other released material in the market and for radio airplay, the final touches are made to smooth mixes over and strengthen various elements in each track, volume fade-outs can be placed at the end and beginning of tracks, and other final adjustments are made to achieve the desired sound. This process creates the final versions of the recordings, typically known as the masters.

Master Use License

A license to make reproductions of master recordings.

Mechanical Rights

A. Broadcast Mechanical

When a song or musical composition is played on television, excluding live performances, two distinct rights are normally involved: the performing right and the mechanical right. The Supreme Court of Canada has ruled that the right to broadcast a performance does not include the right to make a recording of the performance, so there are therefore two distinct rights. Broadcast mechanical rights are technically mechanical rights.

B. Mechanical License

A mechanical license is an agreement between the user and the publisher of the music, which the user intends to reproduce in Canada. The license is normally very specific, limited to a particular composition, as manufactured (or imported) by the user on a particular product. The license also normally specifies the catalogue number of the product, playing time and performer. Note that licenses are not issued per album but rather on a work-by-work basis. If your release contains 10 songs or other works, you must obtain permission for each one. These licenses are issued by the CMRRA and SODRAC on behalf of music publishers in Canada.

C. Mechanical Royalty
Mechanical royalties are amounts paid to a songwriter or composer for the reproduction of a work. For instance, when a record label presses a CD of your song, you are due a mechanical royalty. The ways of dealing with mechanical royalties differ from country to country, and there can be many side deals between bands, labels, and publishers as to royalty rate and how it will be paid. If you have a publishing deal, your publisher will likely receive a percentage of your mechanical royalties before paying them out to you.

Medley
A song or performance that uses portions of other songs and blends them together into a new arrangement.

Merchandise
Merchandise, often called merch, is a blanket term for artist-related goods other than music e.g. T-shirts, posters, etc. Some artist-branded products, e.g. USB sticks, may be both merch and promo.

Metadata
Metadata base applications are used by the majority of music software programs to provide these applications with information about a CD when that CD is inserted into a computer. (Also see Gracenote)

Moral Rights
Rights an author retains over the integrity of a work and the right to be named as its author even after sale or transfer of the copyright. As the primary owners, creators of musical or other works may transfer their economic interest in these works to third parties (e.g., to another

individual or company). However, creators may not transfer or assign their moral rights – although they may choose not to exercise them

Most Favored Nations (MFN)

In the context of music industry agreements, an MFN clause provides that an amount, a definition, or another aspect of a contractual relationship (such as license or royalty fees) will be computed or defined in at least as favorable a manner as the computation or definition given to one or more third parties.

Music Canada

Music Canada is a non-profit trade organization that represents the major record labels in Canada, namely EMI Music Canada, Sony Music Entertainment Canada, Universal Music Canada and Warner Music Canada. Music Canada also provides certain membership benefits to some of the leading independent record labels and distributors. Its members are engaged in all aspects of the recording industry, including the manufacture, production, promotion and distribution of music.

Music Publisher

A music publisher is responsible for ensuring that songwriters and composers receive payment when their compositions are commercially used. Through an agreement called a publishing agreement, a songwriter or composer "assigns" the copyright of their composition to a publishing company. In return, the company licenses compositions, helps monitor where compositions are used, collects royalties and distributes them to the composers. The publishing company normally takes a percentage of income derived from the exploitation of the copyrights.

Music Supervisor

A music supervisor is the person in charge of placing music in films, TV shows, advertising and video games. Clients approach music supervisors with an idea of what kind of music they need for their project (or sometimes even specific ideas of songs they want), and the music supervisor then finds the appropriate music and acts as a liaison between clients and the rights holders of the music. They work to arrange the appropriate licensing for the songs, and work to negotiate licensing deals that come in on budget for their clients.

Musical Work
Any work of music or musical composition, with or without words.

Option (contract)
An option is normally an option to extend the term of a contract but it doesn't mean everybody has options. Sometimes only the label has the option and it may be automatic.

Override
A royalty paid to producers of sound recordings based on the sales of recordings. It is normally a negotiated percentage (usually 1 to 3 points), which is paid by the record label to the producer, either in addition to the Artist's royalty or taken from the Artist's royalty points. In some cases, other parties besides the Producer (i.e. an Investor) may receive a similar royalty.

Performing (Communication) **Right**
One of the rights in the "bundle of rights" that comprises the copyright in a musical work. Specifically, this relates to the public performance of copyrighted musical works (broadcast, live performance) and the communication by telecommunication of musical works (cable TV transmissions, Internet, mobile, satellite, etc.).

Performing Rights Organization (PRO)
An organization that administers the performing rights associated with a musical work, on behalf of composers, lyricists, songwriters and music publishers.

Perpetuity
In the music industry, this term usually means payments with no definitive end.

Personal Manager
A person who assists a musician in the development and management of his music and entertainment career.

Posthumous work
A work, which is published for the first time (or, for certain types of works, performed or delivered in public for the first time) after the author's death.

Private Copying
Copying for personal use, a pre-recorded musical work or a performers' performances of a musical work onto a blank medium, such as an audio tape, cassette, or CD-R.

Producer
The producer is responsible for putting the record/song/album together and making it sellable. This can involve picking out songs or helping the artist with songwriting. A good producer will usually ensure that the songs are acceptable to the record label and for radio as well as see the project through, from pre production to the final mastering stage.

Public Domain (PD)
Materials for which no individual can claim copyright. No license is needed to use public domain materials. For music specifically, works published before 1923 are in the public domain. Music and lyrics published in 1922 or earlier are in the Public Domain in the United States. No one can claim ownership of a song in the public domain; therefore public domain songs may be used by anyone. Sound recordings, however, are protected separately from musical compositions. There are no sound recordings in the Public Domain in

the USA. If you need a sound recording, even a recording of a public domain song you will either have to record it yourself or license one.

Publishing Agreement
A legal contract between a composer/lyricist (author)/songwriter and

a publisher.

Publishing Administrator

A third-party publisher that – for a fixed term –controls all licensing and the collection of publishing revenue streams on behalf of a composer or copyright owner.

Publisher Share

The share of revenues granted to the music publisher via a publishing contract depending on the type of publishing agreement (i.e. songwriter, co-publishing, sub-publishing, administration. Normally, the publisher's share can never exceed 50%. Depending on the type of publishing agreement, a publisher may acquire an "ownership share" in the copyrights for a period of time, including in perpetuity – this being the traditional and most common basis of an agreement. However, the ownership share and the collection share may differ, as in a typical co-publishing agreement.

QR Code

A Quick Response (QR) code is a square barcode used to link people to a specific web address. Users can scan the barcode with a mobile phone-based QR app and it will take the user straight to the URL.

Recoup/Recoupment

Record companies make monetary advances to artists to fund the production and marketing costs of producing a recording, and for concert tours. The record companies then "recoup" these funds from the proceeds of record sales Recoupment is a common practice in the music industry of claiming an advance provided to an artist back from that artist.

Reproduction Right

Under the Copyright Act, the reproduction right gives the copyright owner the exclusive right to authorize the reproduction of music (usually called "mechanical licensing") and in films, TV programs and other audio-visual productions ("synchronization licensing").

RIAA

Recording Industry Association of America. The US based trade group for the recording industry.

Rights Management

The comprehensive, overall administration of copyrights owned by an individual or company, and the resulting revenue streams that deal with copyrighted musical works and/or sound recordings. This may also include the management of rights for other revenue- generating intellectual property, such as logos, names, images and likenesses.

Ringtone/Ringback

A ringtone is the sound (or sounds) that a cellular telephone plays to warn the subscriber that there is an incoming call. A ringback is the sound (or sounds) that a cellular telephone plays to let the listener know that an outgoing call is being made. More often than not, ringtones and ringbacks are excerpts of a musical work.

Royalty

A sum paid to copyright owners for the sale or use of their musical works or other subject matter.

Royalty Participation Agreement

A contract between a copyright owner (i.e. a composer) and a third party (i.e. an investor, producer or non-writing band member). In these contracts, normally the copyright owner agrees to share a percentage of specified royalty streams for a specific period of time under certain terms with others who may have contributed to the success of the copyright, even though these others did create the work(s). The parties have no ownership share in the copyright of the work(s) in question. The royalty payable under these contracts are commonly referred to as the "Loyalty Royalty".

Runner

The runner is responsible for fetching guitar strings, food, drum heads, rented equipment or other items that will assist with the comfort of the artist or smooth operation of the studio or session. They may also be asked to deliver items to places.

Sample (As in sampling a record)
A creative appropriation of a section, piece or element of a copyrighted sound recording and the underlying musical composition. In most cases, the "sample" must be cleared with the copyright owners (i.e.: record label and music publisher), to avoid future infringement claims.

SESAC
Society of European Stage Authors & Composers (but known now just as SESAC) is a performing rights organization in the US.

Shareholder
In the context of music creators, an author, composer, arranger or publisher that owns a percentage of a work.

Small Rights
This refers to the bundle of rights in a musical work comprising performance, communication and reproduction rights (mechanical, synchronization and print). The term 'small rights' normally refers to performing rights that are not grand rights.

Sound Exchange
The US organization, affiliated with the RIAA, which licenses and collects royalties for some digital performances of sound recordings (i.e. on web radio or websites with music).

Sound Recording
In essence, a sound recording is the "sound carrier" – a generic term used for any technology (media) that allows recording to be stored.

Statutory Rate
Federally mandated amount that composers are paid whenever a CD or Digital Download with their song is distributed. This rate is determined by a national committee. Compulsory mechanical law

mandates that copyright holders issue a license at this rate. As of October 2008 the statutory mechanical rate is as follows: 9.1 cents for songs 5 minutes or less and 1.75 cents per minute or fraction thereof over 5 minutes. These rates will remain in effect until December 31, 2012, at which time the national committee will issue a new rate schedule.

Streaming

Streaming is the act of sending and receiving content in a compressed form over the Internet. With streaming video or streaming media, a Web user does not have to wait to download a file to play it. Instead, the media is sent in a continuous stream of data and is played as it arrives. The user needs a player, which is a special program that decompresses and sends video data to the display and audio data to speakers. A player can be either an integral part of a browser or downloaded from the software maker's Web site.

Sub-Publishing Agreement

A foreign publisher that represents the entire catalogue or individual copyrights of another publisher (the "original publisher") in another country. Sub-publishers generally do not have any ownership share and for the most part focus on administration, although creative exploitation may also be undertaken by foreign sub-publishers.

Synchronization ("Sync") Right

The sync right is the right to authorize the recording of a musical work onto the soundtrack of an audio/visual work (film, television program, music video, video game, commercial). A synchronization license is needed for a song to be reproduced and songwriters and publishers receive royalties for sync rights.

Target Audience

A specific group of people at which a product or the marketing message of a product is aimed at. It's important to understand who your most enthusiastic fans are so you can shape your marketing approach and strategies around them.

Trademark
A trademark is a distinctive sign or symbol used by an individual, business organization or legal entity to identify a work, a product or a service, in order to distinguish itself from other entities. A trademark is a type of intellectual property and typically a name, word, phrase, logo, symbol, design or image.

Transformative Use
This refers to the fair use defense (in the US, not Canada); particularly in judicial decisions relating to parody and satire. Transformative use is cited as a reason, which exempts uses "for the purposes of caricature, parody or pastiche". Although these uses are not defined, they allow users to reuse elements of previous works for their own creative or transformative purpose.

UPC
The Universal Product Code (UPC) is a specific type of barcode widely used for tracking products in stores. Its most common form, the UPC-A, consists of 12 numerical digits, which are uniquely assigned to each product.

Viral marketing
Viral marketing describes strategies that encourage individuals to pass on a marketing message to others, creating the potential for exponential growth in the message's exposure and influence. Like viruses, such strategies take advantage of rapid multiplication to explode the message to thousands, or to millions. The goal of successful viral-marketing programs is to identify individuals with high social net

working potential (SNP) and create viral messages that appeal to this segment of the population and have a high probability of being taken by another competitor. Viral marketing has been referred to as "word-of-mouth," "creating a buzz," "leveraging the media" and "network marketing."

Webcast
A webcast is a media file distributed over the Internet using streaming media technology to distribute an audio or video message to many simultaneous listeners/viewers. A webcast may either be distributed live or on demand. Essentially, webcasting is "broadcasting" over the Internet.

Work Registration Form
Declaration of a musical work, including the title, duration and shareholder information such as percentages related to its creators (writer, composer) and to the publisher.

Work for Hire
A work for hire is an exception to the general rule that the person who creates a work is the legally recognized author of that work. Under US copyright law and in some other jurisdictions, if a work is "made for hire", the employer, not the employee is considered the legal author.

Writer Share
The percentage of ownership in a work attributable to the author and/or composer.

Photo Credits

Cover Photo – Andrew "Mr Chrubbs" Ross
Memoir Photos – Malachi Dofat for Refined Pix
And Various